CHERRY AMES' BOOK OF FIRST AID
AND HOME NURSING

CHERRY AMES'
BOOK OF FIRST AID
AND
HOME NURSING

By

HELEN WELLS

~~~~~~

NEW YORK

GROSSET & DUNLAP

Publishers

ACKNOWLEDGEMENT

My thanks to Mrs. Muriel Crothers Henry, Program Director, and Mrs. Sara Wright Kelley, Assistant Director, of the Committee on Careers, National League for Nursing, New York, for their suggestions and valuable help in the preparation of this book.

Thanks are also due Mrs. Marilyn Freedman, Education Director, Helene Fuld School of Practical Nursing, at The Hospital for Joint Diseases, New York, for her generous help with the Cherry Ames books and for information on practical nurse training.

—Helen Wells

Contents

A Letter from Cherry Ames

Dear Reader:

I've always thought of nursing, and perhaps you have, too, as just about the most exciting, important, and rewarding profession there is. Can you think of any other skill that is *always* needed by everybody, everywhere? Doesn't real glamour belong to the girls in white?

Not only can the graduate R.N., in her starched white cap, be of service to others. So can a teen-age nurses' aide, helping with patients in a hospital. But often the most valuable aid comes from the teen-ager who is able and eager to help the people closest to her—her family, friends and neighbors. Often she is in a position to do the things which no one else may have the time or flair to do. You need not be a full-fledged nurse to contribute to the health and happiness of your family.

1

If you ever have had someone sick at your house, you will know how many things must be done—quickly, efficiently, and quietly—to ensure a speedy and complete recovery.

Or if you have ever witnessed an accident, even a minor one, and seen bystanders floundering around in their well-meaning ignorance—well, it's something you just don't forget. Perhaps it has sent you, or will, to your Red Cross or Y or school for a course in first aid.

Have you ever cut your thumb or sprained your ankle? If you have, you know how serious and awkward even a "small" injury can be. Unless someone gives prompt good care, you can end up with a serious infection or a painful limp.

I don't mean to sound gloomy. Indeed, like any nurse, I think the best kind of health care is that which *keeps* us fit as a fiddle.

If I've mentioned only a few of the nursing and first-aid problems you may be called upon to deal with right now, think of how much more skill you will need when you are grown-up—when you have a family of your own to keep well and strong and happy. Whatever you can learn now will prove as useful then as it is today.

Besides, helping in nursing situations is fun!

Did I hear someone mention chores, and groan about working around the house? Granted, dusting a room or changing beds aren't the most romantic jobs in the world. But they do ensure cleanliness. Someone—someone interested, intelligent, knowledgeable—is needed to do them. You see, most specialized nursing techniques are only a part of the health picture. Beyond that, there is so much that you can do to provide for the comfort and well-being of the patient. Ask any nurse. Once you get into the swing of it, helping *can* be fun.

Some girls, while still quite young, already know that nursing is the career for them. If you are thinking about an R.N. after your name in the future—or if you want to become a teen-age nurses' aide in your spare time—any nursing experience you undertake now will help you to build your future.

But whether you eventually become a nurse or not, you are always needed to play an important part in the care of others. You will use your feminine skills not only to nurse the sick, but to also meet everyday needs and emergencies. You will be able to take pride in your responsibilities, and in what you can accomplish for your family and friends, and —surprisingly—for yourself. You will discover that you are important and needed.

I hope you will really use this book. And I hope you'll enjoy reading and using it as much as I have in writing it.

CHAPTER I

Emergency!

HAVE YOU EVER SEEN AN ACCIDENT HAPPEN BEFORE your very eyes?

Do you know that most accidents occur—of all places—at home?

Do you know what *you* can do to help someone who is injured?

For example, if you have a brother (as I have), you know he is likely to do such stunts as climbing the highest tree or walking the porch railing. Most times he is sure-footed. But what about the one time he slips and falls—and lies helpless on the ground? He is cut, bruised, stunned, and for all you can tell, may have hurt himself badly.

If your mother is at home, she will need your help. Suppose, though, that your mother is out when your brother gets hurt.

The first thing you should do is to call a doctor. Telephone *promptly*. If you delay, the injury has time in which to grow more serious.

5

WHERE TO GET HELP

Where can you get a doctor—a reliable doctor—and quickly? If your family has a family doctor, whom you consult regularly, of course you will call him. Failing that, or if he is out, you may know of a good doctor in your neighborhood who has been recommended by your school nurse, or a neighbor. Call him.

In case you don't happen to know the name of a doctor, or aren't sure, then ask your local hospital. Your telephone operator can help you. Just tell her, "I want a doctor. Please connect me with the nearest hospital." Every hospital has doctors and internes and at least one ambulance on call, to go out quickly to meet emergencies.

If you need a nurse, call (or ask the telephone operator to call) a nurses' registry. A registry lists the names and addresses of graduate nurses who will come to your home. Or if you need a nurse only for an hour or so, call your Visiting Nurse Service.

There are many people and organizations ready to help you in case you need them. No matter where you live, or what time of day or night it is, you can always get help. You already know about your doctor and your hospital. You can also rely on your police department and fire department. They exist in order to help you. They have rescue squads. So don't be afraid to call if you need help in an emergency.

Once, when my twin brother Charlie and I were ten years old, we visited our grandparents' farm and had a fine time climbing the giant oaks. Naturally

Charlie climbed to the very top of the tallest tree. While he was up there, he wrenched his wrist and then tore the skin off his palms so badly that he couldn't shinny down again. Nobody was on the farm that day who could climb up to rescue him. It was unsafe for Charlie to jump from that height.

What to do? We telephoned our local fire department. They came with ladders, and a skillful fireman carried him down—much to Charlie's embarrassment!

Then, besides your local hospital, police and fire departments, there are the large national organizations. Everyone knows the Red Cross, which gives magnificent help in times of floods or tornados or other public emergency, as well as day-to-day work. Of course you know of Civil Defense, and perhaps you have visited its branch in your town.

However, not all of the people who are ready to help you are—or need to be—professionals. Often they are your neighbors and your own parents, trained and serving as volunteer firemen and volunteer first-aid workers. It isn't always possible to have a great many professionals or elaborate equipment. Many times you and your family and neighbors can help yourselves in an emergency with your own skills. And one of the most self-reliant and helpful of these people may well be yourself.

WHAT DOCTORS AND NURSES DO

Of course, no one but a doctor can treat a seriously injured or sick person properly. Even the best-trained volunteer cannot replace a doctor or nurse—although he or she can give vital help.

When I was nurse-in-charge at a girls' boarding school, an automobile accident happened one day just outside our gate. Everyone in the school heard the crash and rushed out to the road. A young football player and his coach were in the car which had hit a tree, and they were hurt. Of course the first thing we did was to call our doctor.

Everyone was wonderfully helpful. The students realized they must *not* crowd around, in order to give the injured men air and quiet. Two women teachers helped me to staunch some bleeding, and we loosened tight collars, shoe laces and belts. I was glad at that moment I happened to be a nurse! The men teachers quickly brought blankets and a warm stimulating drink. We didn't move the men until the doctor arrived and decided what to do. When Dr. Wilcox came, he gave both men preventive injections. Then he instructed us to move the coach gently to the one stretcher we had prepared and then the football player. With careful nursing overnight in our school infirmary and later in the hospital, both of them made a good recovery. But you can be sure that doing the right thing in the first few minutes after the accident, with everybody helping and co-operating, was decisive in their getting well.

AT YOUR HOUSE

Suppose an accident or unexpected illness happens at your house, in your family. What can you do to help your mother and father?

I. CALL A DOCTOR.

Don't delay. You will want to tell the doctor where the injured or ill person is, what has happened to him, and the extent of the illness or injury.

2. KEEP CALM.

An excited person usually doesn't exercise good judgment. She doesn't get much or the right thing accomplished. Remember, it's as important for a first aider to know what *not* to do, as to know what she should do. Don't let those who are excited disturb you. If you keep calm, you'll be more efficient and get more done in the end. Besides, your attitude will help the patient to cooperate.

3. WHEN NOT TO MOVE THE PATIENT.

Don't move him if there is any chance that he or she may have broken a bone. Don't move him if the patient shows signs of shock or internal injuries. Don't move a patient who has a head injury.

This is how you can tell if the patient has broken (fractured) a bone: He will usually be in some pain. The skin on top of the injured part will be sore, will soon swell, and may turn red or purplish. The patient cannot move the injured arm or leg or part. It may seem to be out of shape or in an awkward position. Sometimes you will see only one, or two, of these symptoms. If you move him, the sharp ends of the broken bone may injure muscles and veins. Or the broken bone may puncture the skin. Don't move the patient, and gently prevent him from moving.

This is how you can tell if the patient shows signs of shock: His face is white or pale. Even his ears and nails may look gray or bluish. He has cold sweat on his forehead and palms, and he is cold, perhaps shivering. His breathing is shallow and irregular. His pulse is fast and weak. He is exhausted and sometimes feels nauseated. If he is not lying down, you should assist him to do so. Remember that any type of serious injury may cause shock.

This is how you can tell if the patient has internal injuries: He shows signs of shock and pain. There may or may not be bleeding.

As for a head injury, you may be able to see it. The patient may bleed from his ears. Generally the patient is unconscious or half-conscious, after a severe blow on his head.

Never give a drink of water or anything else to swallow to an unconscious person. It will choke him.

In general, or if you aren't sure, it is safest to keep an injured person lying down. Keep his head level with his body. *Don't move him,* and don't let him get up. This will prevent the patient from fainting or falling.

Whatever you do, don't rush. Go slowly and carefully. Handle the patient gently and as little as possible.

However, here are three exceptions when it is important for you to act promptly. These are: 1) when the patient is bleeding much or steadily; 2) when the patient stops breathing; and 3) when he is poisoned, in that order of importance. In these cases, the very first thing you should do—yes, even before call-

ing the doctor—is to give the correct first-aid measures. (We'll talk about these in detail later.)

4. WARMTH AND COMFORT ARE IMPORTANT.

Whether he is lying down or resting in a chair, you
can gently cover your patient with a blanket or coat.
Keeping warm is especially important for a person
who feels chilly from shock.

If the weather is cold, tuck the blanket around the
patient as well. You may need to use more than one
blanket if the weather is very cold. But try to choose
coverings which are light in weight, and will not
press heavily on the patient. Be careful not to cover
the patient so much that he sweats—just comfortably warm, please.

5. REASSURE YOUR PATIENT.

A cheerful word or a little encouragement can help
him a great deal. You won't have to say too much—
in fact, *too* much talk can disturb your patient. If
you are cheerful, calm, hopeful, you will really help
him.

Sometimes a sick or injured person is frightened,
though he may not show it. Be sure to tell him that
you are getting a doctor and that you will do all you
can to help him.

6. HOW AND WHERE IS HE HURT?

It is a good idea to ask the patient to tell you, when
he is able to do so, how he was injured or taken sick.
Try to learn what sort of pain or discomfort he feels,
and where. You will then know what to report to

the doctor, and how best to help your patient until the doctor comes.

If the patient is too badly hurt to tell you, then try to locate the injury yourself. When you examine him or her, do it gently and cautiously. If you must remove clothing, push it aside or cut it away. Removing clothing in the usual way can cause further injury.

Be sure to check whether the patient has more than one injury. Be sure to give first-aid measures to all of them, if necessary. After you give first aid then you can see about moving the patient.

If you can, try not to let the patient see his or her own injury. It may upset him or make him feel faint.

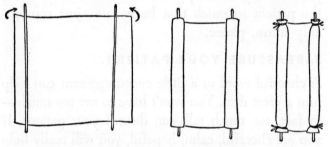

1. Place poles along each short edge of open blanket.
2. Roll poles toward middle of blanket to desired width.
3. Tie ends of poles securely to blanket.

7. HOW TO CARRY A PATIENT.

When you find it necessary to carry someone hurt or ill (*excepting* cases of fractures, shock, internal injury, and head injury), the safest way is to use a stretcher. Or use an improvised stretcher which you can make yourself.

To make a stretcher, you'll need two sturdy poles

and a blanket or rug or strong sheet. A blanket is best
1.) Spread out the blanket and place one pole on
each short edge. 2.) Now roll the poles toward the
middle until the stretcher is as wide as you want it.
3.) Tie the ends of the blanket securely into place.

Never attempt to lift or roll a patient onto a
stretcher by yourself. You may drop the patient, and
you may strain yourself. This is a job for grown ups.
Several men may be needed to lift an injured man
safely.

There is a two-man carry by extremities, but do
not use this if you suspect your patient has fractured
a bone. There is also an eight-man hand carry.
Then, too, a chair may be used as a litter. But you
need considerable strength and practice to manage
any of these. It's safer to have adults carry the ill or
injured person.

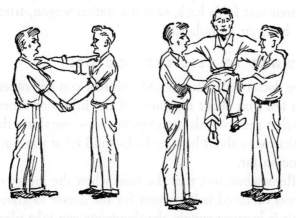

Two-man Carry: Face partner. Grasp his left shoulder with right hand, as his left hand grasps your right
shoulder. Clasp free hands. To pick up patient, carriers
bend knees on clasped-hands side.

The "walking assist" is useful when the patient is not too seriously ill or injured, and is able to walk. Put your left arm around his waist, to support him, and draw his right arm around your shoulders. Let him lean on you. Walk slowly and gently with him. Pause and rest often to conserve his strength.

A fireman's rescue trick is this: Place the victim on a coat or blanket, then drag the blanket along. (This requires the strength of at least two children—don't try it all by yourself.) The floor or ground must be smooth and not uphill, otherwise the victim will not stay on the blanket.

One word of warning: "Jack knifing" an injured person into a car, and then speeding to the hospital, can hurt him still more. Here is a safer way: If your patient is short enough, you can use the back seat as a bed. For a taller person, either improvise a bed, if a front seat folds back, or use a station wagon, truck or, best, an ambulance.

8. WHAT TO TELL THE DOCTOR.

The doctor will want to know all that you and others can tell him about the cause of the injury or illness —what the wounds or symptoms are—anything the patient says about how he feels—and what you have done so far.

Remember, too, that the time when the injury or illness occurred is important for the doctor to know. This is because certain developments can take place rapidly.

When the doctor asks you questions, you'll of

course give him the most accurate, concise answers that you can.

The doctor will instruct you on what supplies to have on hand. Write down the items he names. These are important if you are to do a first-rate home nursing job. Then take your list and the doctor's prescriptions promptly to a reliable pharmacy. Get exactly what you were told to get.

Eight-man Carry: Four carriers line up on each side of patient, each kneeling on knee away from patient's head. Slip hands under neck, shoulders, back, buttocks, thighs and legs. Rise in unison.

Possibly you already have on hand several of the things which the doctor requests. In most people's homes, and I'm sure at your house, Mother keeps ready several essentials: medications, bandages, and other supplies.

One of the most convenient ways to do this is to

have a first-aid kit. Is there one in your house? Do you have a kit of your own?

CHERRY SAYS

Call the doctor promptly if an accident or illness occurs at your house.

Keep calm. Remember that a good first aider knows what to do—and what not to do.

Watch for any sign of shock. Keep your patient lying down, warm and comfortable.

Be cheerful, and reassure your patient.

Don't give an unconscious patient anything to drink or swallow.

Don't move a patient who may have a fracture, who shows signs of shock, or who has head or internal injuries.

Immediately, even before you call the doctor, give first aid to a person who is bleeding seriously, who has stopped breathing, or who is poisoned. You may save a life if you act promptly.

Don't try to lift a patient by yourself. Ask adults to help.

Learn all the facts you can about the injury or illness, and report these facts to the doctor.

When the doctor arrives, cooperate with him and follow his instructions exactly.

CHAPTER II

How to Make a First-Aid Kit

EVERY HOUSEHOLD SHOULD BE SURE TO HAVE A FIRST-aid kit. Does your house have one? Is it completely stocked? Are the supplies fresh and clean?

You need a first-aid kit for treating many different kinds of small emergencies, everything from a scratch on the arm to a mild nosebleed. You will also find your first-aid kit essential in case of more serious emergencies, to help *in certain cases* while you are waiting for an adult or a doctor or nurse to give fuller treatment.

Perhaps you already own a first-aid kit through your Girl Scout troop, and know how to use it. Now is a good time to check through your kit and replenish it.

If you would like to make a first-aid kit for your family, or for your own use, here is a good way to do it:

First, get a good-sized box—clean and sturdy—with a lid. A tin box or a wooden cigar box are good choices. If you wish, you can paint the box to improve its appearance.

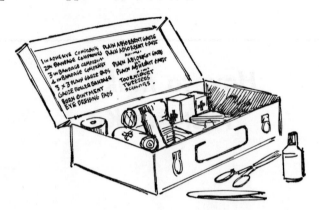

WHAT TO PUT IN A FIRST-AID KIT

What goes into a first-aid kit? There are several kinds for various uses. Naturally the one you keep on hand at home will be the most complete. It should contain most or, if possible, all of the following things:

1 small bottle of antiseptic (germ-killer, either iodine or peroxide.) Remember that iodine and peroxide are poisonous if anyone drinks them. The label must state this.

1 small tube of sterile petrolatum ointment, such as vaseline

1 small bottle of aromatic spirits of ammonia

1 box of bicarbonate of soda

1 box of boric acid powder, and a medicine dropper. Some medicine droppers come in their own tubes.

1 small tube of calamine ointment (non-greasy)

When you buy these medications at the drugstore, buy small, even tiny quantities. Then replenish them as needed. Your supplies must be fresh to be effective. Also be sure that each item is clearly labeled.

Your first-aid kit will also need:

1 small box adhesive bandages or plastic strips individually wrapped

1 or 2 sterile gauze squares, about 3 x 3 inches, in individual wrappers

1 roll of sterile bandage gauze, 2 or 3 inches wide, in a sealed package

1 triangular bandage to use as a sling

1 small roll of sterile absorbent cotton, boxed

1 small package of short wooden applicators tipped with sterile cotton

1 small roll adhesive tape

1 pair of small blunt bandage scissors

2 fine steel needles, and safety (kitchen) matches

1 small box of wooden tongue depressors

You probably already have at your house other necessary items such as a thermometer (preferably in its own tube), a hot water bag and an ice bag. A flashlight, particularly a small one, is a useful item to have, too. Tweezers often come in handy.

MAKE A LIST FOR YOUR KIT

Now that you have assembled all these items, your next question is how to arrange everything in the box in the best—and most convenient—way. First, which items do you think you will use most often? Probably the antiseptic, cotton, adhesive bandages and vaseline. You'll want to put these on top, or wherever you decide is the most convenient place.

You'll find it's handy to write or type a list of the contents and paste this inside the lid of the box. Then you, or anyone who needs to use the kit, can see at a glance what he or she will find in it. You'll also find the list useful when you check, from time to time, to make sure your supplies are fresh and complete.

WHERE TO KEEP YOUR KIT

If a first-aid kit is planned for your entire family, best keep it downstairs or in a room where everyone can get to it. But also place it on a high shelf, out of reach of your small brothers and sisters. Explain to them why they must not touch the kit and its contents.

Your own personal kit will be a useful addition to the family supplies. You may wish to talk over with your mother the best location for it. In or near the medicine cabinet is often a convenient spot. Isn't your family in the habit of looking there for iodine or an aspirin?

YOUR FAMILY MEDICAL SUPPLIES

Besides your first-aid kit, you should keep a small, fresh, clean supply of these suggested things in your family medicine chest. Perhaps you already have these items on hand. You might like to talk over this list with your mother, and decide whether it suits *your* family's needs.

1 tube of sterile petroleum jelly (such as vaseline)
1 roll of adhesive tape, with a self-cutting container
1 small box of absorbent cotton (Keep it tightly closed.)
A few packages of finger dressings (such as adhesive
   bandages or plastic strips)
A few sterile gauze squares, for dressings
A few gauze bandages of different widths (or clean
   white cotton cloth cut into strips)
A pair of blunt scissors, for making bandages
A pair of tweezers, for removing splinters
1 thermometer (preferably in its own tube)
1 medicine glass, marked to show amounts
1 medicine dropper

Your doctor may suggest a few medications, such
as an antiseptic, or an ointment for burns, or a lotion for insect bites in summer.

Be sure to keep drugs and medicines separate
from tooth powder and mouthwash. Drugs and medicines are powerful, and may even be poisonous if
taken by mistake. Keep them on a high shelf by
themselves.

TRAVELER'S FIRST-AID KIT

It's a good idea for anyone who starts out on a hike,
a picnic, or a trip to take along a pocket-size first-
aid kit. Here again you can make your own.

Start with an envelope or flat square purse made
of a waterproof material. You might use a roll-up
transparent pouch such as men use for pipe tobacco.
Be sure your kit is clean. Into it you can put:

A few individually wrapped adhesive bandages or plastic
   strips
1 small, tightly capped tube of vaseline

1 small, tightly capped bottle of iodine or peroxide
1 small sealed package of sterile cotton
1 fine steel needle. Borrow rather than carry matches
   if you need them to sterilize the needle.

If you belong to a Girl Scout troop, school club, or church group which goes on hikes or cookouts, a larger first-aid kit than your personal one might well go along, too.

Whether at home or away, you will be better able to take care of bumps and bruises with a well-equipped first aid kit on hand to help you.

CHERRY SAYS

Do you have a first-aid kit at home?

Does every member of your family know where it is kept?

Is it well-stocked with all the necessary items?

Do you and your family replace antiseptics, ointments, bandages, etc. as they are used up?

Are all the items arranged for easy use, with those most used on top?

Is your family's first-aid kit out of reach of younger brothers and sisters?

Is there one in the family car?

CHAPTER III

Bandages and Dressings

IT'S AMAZING HOW MANY WAYS THERE ARE IN which you can use the squares of gauze and the tightly packed roll of bandage from your first-aid kit in an emergency. But to apply them skillfully takes a bit of practice. Shall we try? Once you've mastered the various techniques, you'll be ready to care for your brother's scratched knee or a wrenched ankle with equal ease.

To begin with, a dressing is a compress, or folded thickness of gauze, which you place directly on a wound. A bandage or adhesive tape is used to hold it firmly in place.

The first and most important thing you'll want to check about any bandage and dressing is whether they are clean and sterile. Sterile means free from germs. As you know, germs or live bacteria can cause infection and illness. Be especially careful not to let germs come in contact with a scratch or any other open wound.

You'll notice that supplies which you buy in the drugstore come tightly sealed. This is to protect the sterilized dressings and bandages from the dirt and bacteria which we often carry on our hands.

CLEAN AND STERILE, PLEASE

Be sure your hands are clean before you touch a dressing or bandage. The best way to wash your hands thoroughly is with hot running water and soap. Then dry your hands on a clean towel. (Paper towels, used once and thrown away, are sanitary.)

Be sure, too, when you unwrap the sterile dressing, not to set it down or let it touch anything which is not clean and sterile. Hold the dressing by its corners, so that your fingers will not touch the part that will cover the wound. Don't even breathe on it.

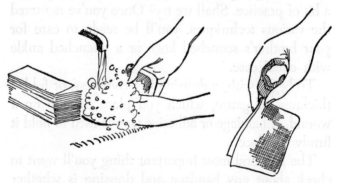

Always wash your hands thoroughly before handling a dressing. Hold the dressing by its corner.

AN EMERGENCY DRESSING

Suppose you are at home when your younger sister accidentally cuts her finger on the scissors. You want to treat her promptly. But just this once you can't find a sterile dressing or adhesive bandage. It is a long way to the drugstore or to the doctor's, and her finger is bleeding. In that case, you might take a clean, soft, white handkerchief or cloth. Wash it quickly in soap and water. Laundering will kill bacteria. Then wring the cloth out *dry*. Later you can change this emergency dressing and bandage for a sterile one.

A SPECIAL WORD ABOUT DRESSINGS

What size dressing will you decide to use? A dressing should be large enough to cover the entire wound, with an inch or so to overlap.

Your druggist has on hand sterile gauze squares of several thicknesses, about 3½ x 3½ inches. You will find these convenient for small wounds, and you can of course fold the dressing to the right size.

You can also buy a thicker, larger bandage compress which opens out to almost any size you may need. Or you can buy a roll of sterilized gauze and fold a length of this into a dressing—but once the roll is opened, you can't be sure that it will remain sterile. Then, too, an adhesive compress—for example, an adhesive bandage or plastic strip—is a dressing. Easy to apply, either type is an excellent first-aid item to have on hand.

Do not use either cotton or adhesive tape in direct contact with a wound. These materials will stick as the wound heals and closes. It is then difficult and painful to remove them. Your best material for dressings and bandages is sterile white gauze.

MANY KINDS OF BANDAGES

How many kinds of bandages do you suppose there are? Why so many kinds?

When I was a student nurse at Spencer Hospital, Dr. Wylie used to remark that "Human beings are built in a fairly complicated design." You'll admit that a bandage shaped to fit your finger won't fit or stay on your knee. Another reason for the variety in bandages: Do you need the bandage to support a broken arm, or is it to protect a burned area of skin? Or is it to help stop bleeding? Or to hold a dressing in place?

You can become skillful at making all kinds of bandages, if you'll practice doing it. In nursing school, Gwen Jones and Ann Evans and I used to practice by bandaging one another. We laughed about applying bandages to our perfectly healthy selves, but later on in emergencies our practice came in handy.

A SPECIAL WORD ABOUT BANDAGES

Remember that *first* you place a sterile dressing over the wound, and *then* you apply the bandage. The bandage holds the compress in place.

You will want to be sure that the bandage is not too tight. A too tight bandage is uncomfortable. It can also cut off the blood supply. Just keep the bandage comfortably snug.

One way to tell if the bandage is too tight is if the skin around it starts to look puffy or bluish. Check and see. Remember not to cover up the ends of fingers or toes, unless the injury is there. (Circulation stops first in your fingers and toes. That's why your fingertips grow numb on a frosty day or your foot "goes to sleep.") Loosen the bandage if you decide it is too tight.

Never apply a wet bandage, because it will shrink and pinch as it dries.

To fasten a bandage in place, you tie the ends of the bandage. Tie knots where you can reach them easily. Try to tie a small, smooth, square knot rather than a large, bumpy one which might be awkward for your patient.

When you apply a bandage, keep it simple so it will be easy for the doctor to remove. Do not waste the doctor's time with a complicated bandage or elaborate knots.

SQUARE KNOTS

Follow these steps and the illustrations:

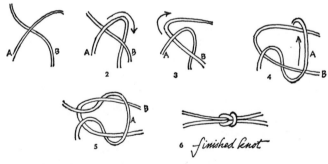

1. Cross bandage ends, with A over B.
2. Loop A down over B.
3. Draw end B to right above knot.
4. Bring A up and over B to top of knot.
5. Slip same end of A through loop.
6. Pull knot tight.

I find it helps, in tying a square knot, to think of it as two V's lying on their sides and interlocked.

CHERRY SAYS

1. Why must a bandage and dressing be sterile and clean?
2. What should you always do before you dress a wound?
3. Which do you place directly over the wound—the dressing or the bandage?
4. How do you hold a dressing?
5. How can you tell if a bandage is too tight?
6. Why is a wet bandage never used?
7. Can you tie a square knot?

CHAPTER IV

The Art of Bandaging

NOW THAT WE KNOW A BIT ABOUT BANDAGES AND dressings, let's try our hand at some of the different bandages that you might be called upon to make. It's fun to practice while you read along. So why not take turns with a friend on trying out your skills?

HOW TO MAKE A TRIANGULAR BANDAGE

If you are a Girl Scout, or have had a first-aid course at school, you know that a triangular bandage is useful and easy to make. If you don't happen to have lengths of gauze on hand, you can tear an old shirt or sheet or even fold a large handkerchief to make a triangular bandage. A good material to use is unbleached muslin. You will need a large piece, about 36 or 40 inches square, or larger to use on adults. By cutting the square diagonally into two pieces, you will have two bandages.

Now let's see the many ways you can use a triangular bandage.

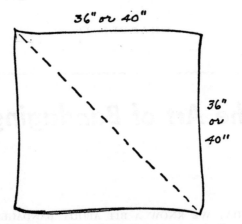

To make a triangular bandage, cut a piece of muslin diagonally. You can use one piece as a triangular bandage, the other for a cravat bandage.

HAND OR FOOT BANDAGE

When I was nurse at Blue Water, a girls' summer camp, one of our farm neighbors, young Mrs. Vernie Epler, upset a kettle of hot water and scalded her foot quite badly. I happened to be visiting in her kitchen when the accident happened, and was able to treat and then bandage her foot. For this I made a triangular bandage out of a clean white cloth, as follows:

First, of course, you place a dressing on the injured foot.

Then you spread out the triangle and place the injured foot in the center of the triangle. Do this so that the heel faces the widest part of the triangle, and the toes face the middle point. Now lift the point of the triangle over the toes and foot, and hold it at the ankle. Bring the remaining ends forward and across the instep. Then bring the ends around the ankle, and tie them over the instep. If you will look at the illustration, you will see exactly how I bandaged Vernie's ankle.

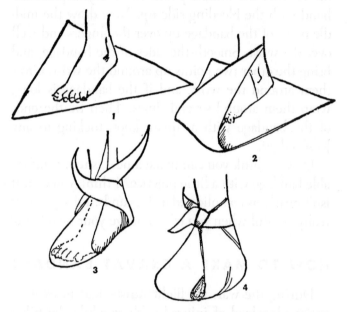

1. Place foot in center of triangle, toes facing center point. 2. Lift point of triangle over toes to ankle. 3. Cross two remaining ends up and over instep. 4. Bring ends around to back of ankle, cross and tie above instep.

(Of course we called our camp doctor at once. First aid, even when a registered nurse like myself gives it, can never take the place of a doctor's diagnosis and treatment.)

When you bandage a hand which has been cut or burned or infected, you use a triangular bandage in much the same way as you do for a foot. To bandage a hand, first place a dressing over the injury. Spread out the triangle and place the hand on it, so that the wrist faces the widest part of the triangle, and the fingers face the middle point. Be sure you place the hand with the bleeding side *up*. Now draw the middle point of the bandage up over the fingers and well over the wrist. Smooth the sides of the bandage, and bring the other two points up around the wrist. Cross them around the wrist, and if the bandage is long, wrap them around several times. Then tie the ends of the bandage with a square knot, tucking in any loose edges.

Do you think you can make a neat, snug, comfortable bandage with a little practice? I think you can. It isn't nearly as complicated as it sounds. I'd say you're really skillful when you can bandage your own hand!

HOW TO MAKE A CRAVAT BANDAGE

During the war, we flight nurses had to treat an entire planeload of injured soldiers while the pilots flew us over dangerous territory, back to an Army hospital. My corpsman and good friend, Bunce, gave me fine assistance in our hospital plane. You can be sure we used the quickest and most efficient methods we knew. One of these is our old friend, the triangular bandage, folded this time as a cravat. You will see in a moment how very many uses a cravat can have.

A cravat bandage looks something like a man's

necktie. To make it, spread out your triangular bandage and fold in the middle point, then fold over twice again—just as in the illustration. Now you have a long, narrow, firm bandage.

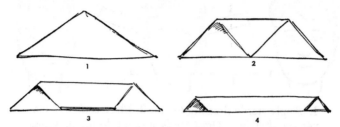

To make cravat bandage, fold center point of triangle to opposite edge. Fold over twice more.

HEAD BANDAGE

Sometimes, when your patient has a bleeding wound on his head or forehead, it is rather hard to stop the bleeding. You'll find the cravat bandage a great help here. First, apply a sterile dressing or compress to the wound. Then place the center of the cravat over the compress. Draw the ends around the head, cross them, and bring them back to the starting point to make a neat square knot. If you need to apply pressure to stop the bleeding, pull the bandage tight as you cross the ends. After the bleeding stops, you can loosen the bandage and make your patient more comfortable.

A head wound sounds like something for only doctors to treat. But a child who falls off a bicycle or trips in a baseball game can receive a cut which bleeds stubbornly. He'll need first aid until a doctor can treat him. You may be the person who can staunch the bleeding, with a sterile dressing and skillful use of your cravat bandage.

1. Apply sterile dressing to cut. 2. Place center of cravat on dressing. Draw ends around head. 3. Cross ends. Bring them back to starting point. Tie.

ELBOW OR KNEE BANDAGE

Where do children bang and scrape themselves most often? Their knees, of course. If you baby sit or have younger sisters or brothers, you'll find plenty of use for this ingenious bandage. It is a good thing to know in many other cases, too.

One evening when I was a student nurse at Spencer Hospital, I was startled to see my pal, Gwen Jones, climb blithely through the open window of my room. It was two minutes after the retiring bell and Gwen, who'd gone out to mail a letter, was locked out of the student nurses' residence. "It's a lucky thing your room is on the ground floor," Gwen told me. Then she said, "Ouch!" We examined her and found she had scraped both knees and her right elbow, badly enough to need thorough cleansing and medication (I had iodine) and bandaging. That evening, I put *three* bandages of this kind on Gwen.

The technique is the same for knee or elbow.

First, be sure to have the patient *bend* his elbow, so that as you wind the bandage, it will have enough "give" to allow your patient to move about freely. Put a sterile dressing on the injured elbow and hold it there as you apply a bandage. As you work, the bandage itself will hold the dressing in place.

Fold your cravat 8 inches wide or wider. Place the middle of the cravat over the elbow—the hollow of the elbow. Smooth it around the bent elbow to fit snugly and bring the ends around several times. Tie them in the hollow of the arm. The illustration shows you exactly how to do this.

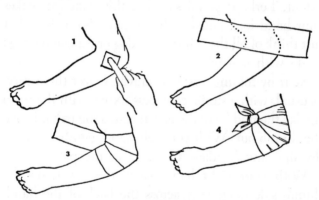

1. Apply dressing to wound. 2. Place cravat across hollow of elbow. 3. Smooth both ends of cravat several times around elbow. 4. Tie ends in hollow of arm.

For the knee, fold your cravat still wider. Then follow the same technique.

PALM OF HAND BANDAGE

Have you ever seen a thoughtless boy with a jackknife, blades open, balancing it or even closing it on the palm of his hand? Have you ever seen someone in the kitchen take hold of a panhandle minus a potholder with her bare hand, not knowing or forgetting that the pan was hot? Or have you ever had a porcelain faucet break in your hand, as I did once when I turned off the water too hard and suddenly? (It was my own fault, for being in such a hurry.) I hope you haven't, because mishaps like these cut or burn the palm. And nothing inconveniences you quite so much as an injured hand.

Fortunately, we have a bandage which, while it protects the palm, allows you to use your hand to some extent. Perhaps you'll say that this bandage makes your hand look and feel like a paw. So it does, but just think of all the things your dog or cat can manage to do with a paw!

Start by folding a narrow cravat. Cover the injury, as usual, with a sterile compress. Now, with the palm up, lay the middle of the cravat across the palm. Leave the thumb out. With your left hand, gently hold the dressing and bandage in place on the palm.

With your right hand, carry the cravat on the thumb side diagonally across the back of the hand. Then from the base of the little finger, bring it diagonally across the palm, to the space between thumb and index finger. Leave it there while you proceed to the next step.

Next, take the other end of the cravat and draw it across the back of the hand to the base of the thumb, then across the palm to the little finger. Now bring it around and across the back of the hand again, but this time bring it between thumb and index finger.

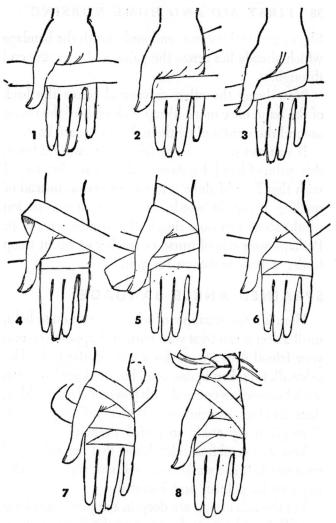

1. Place bandage on palm. 2. Draw left end of bandage to rear of hand and (3.) up under thumb. 4. Next, bring right end across back of hand and over wrist. 5. Repeat, this time bringing right end up under thumb. Slip under loose left end and (6.) under bandage at wrist. 7. Now cross ends at back of hand. 8. Tie at wrist.

Slip or weave this cravat-end underneath the bandage which already lies across the palm, and draw the end through.

Now bring the other cravat-end across the back of the hand once more. Wrap both ends of the cravat around the wrist and tie them. Use a square knot.

If you can weave, drape fabrics, or even tie bows, this palm-of-hand bandage will be easy for you. I wish that I could show it to you in person instead of spelling it out in words, because a demonstration would show you how simple this bandage really is. Perhaps your school nurse or teacher or Scout troop leader will demonstrate for you.

SPRAINED ANKLE BANDAGE

Here is a fine example of what you can do to help, until a doctor can treat your patient. Suppose you and your friend Ann are out for a walk in the park. The sidewalk is broken in one spot, but neither of you can see it because it is covered with leaves. All of a sudden, Ann stumbles, exclaims—and can't walk any farther. "I've given my ankle an awful wrench!"

You, as a good first-aider, know that her ankle will soon swell. If she walks on it, without support, walking will be painful and harmful.

Yet the two of you are deep in the park. You *have* to walk in order to go home or to the doctor's office. Ann is groaning and is no help at all. How can you help her? You're fairly certain that it is a sprain, rather than a fracture. There are signs of swelling, common in both cases. But the limb is not misshapen and the ankle is not red or purplish.

Probably one of you is wearing a scarf or a large kerchief. Take this and fold it into a long, narrow cravat. Leave Ann's shoe on. If it happens to have laces or zipper, loosen them. This is to allow for the ankle to swell.

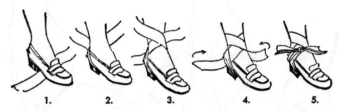

1. Place middle of cravat under shoe's instep. 2. Draw ends back, crossing them behind ankle. 3. Bring ends forward and cross over instep. 4. Slip crossed ends under bandage at shoe's heel. 5. Draw ends forward and tie over instep.

Now place the middle of the cravat under the shoe, right in front of the shoe's heel. Bring the cravat ends up to the back of the ankle, and crisscross them as you draw them forward to the front of the ankle. Cross the ends again over the instep. Bring them down toward the arch of the foot. Then slip each end under the heel bandage which is already in place. Now pull the end so that the bandage is snug. Bring the ends up across the instep again, and tie them.

You have now given your patient a support for her sprained ankle so that she will be able to walk.

ROLLER BANDAGES

Because fingers and toes are small and irregular in shape, doctors often use roller bandages. These

are 1-inch, 2-inch, or 3-inch strips of sterilized gauze.
They come about 5 to 10 yards to each sealed package.
You can cut off whatever length you'll need. (Similar
to rollers are folded or pleated bandages.)

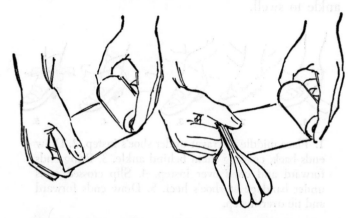

You can make your own pleated bandages by looping
gauze as you strip off desired length of material.

Be cautious when you apply a roller bandage.
If you wind it too tightly around the patient's finger
or toe, you may cut off the circulation. Remember,
too, that the finger or toe probably will swell, so leave
the bandage loose enough to allow for this.

But then this spiral bandage may be so loose it
will fall off. You'll need ingenuity in using adhesive
tape to anchor it. One way to remedy this is to place
adhesive tape at any place where the bandage sags.
(If the result begins to look like a jigsaw puzzle,
don't worry about it.) Another good way to hold this
small, loose bandage in place is to tape the last turn.

In case you have no adhesive tape, here is how to
tie a knot which won't slip: Split the ends of the

bandage into two 4- or 5-inch lengths. Tie a small knot, to keep the bandage from splitting any more. Then bring the ends around the finger or toe, in opposite directions, and tie with a square knot.

FINGER OR TOE BANDAGE

Now that you know how to use a roller bandage, here is the way to bandage an injured finger or toe:

You'll find it best to use a 1-inch bandage. Place your patient's hand with palm down, sore finger extended. Start by wrapping the bandage twice in the same spot, to anchor it. Then wrap it in a close spiral around the length of the finger. The illustration will show you how it should look. Use the same technique for an injured toe.

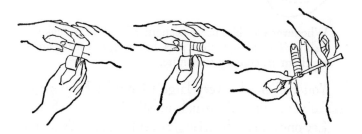

1. Wrap bandage twice round in same spot. 2. Spiral bandage down toward fingertip. 3. Wind bandage back to starting point. Split bandage end and tie.

Don't you agree that this is a miniature version of the forearm bandage we talked about a few pages earlier?

SLINGS

A sling is really a cradle, when you come to think about it. It supports a broken or injured arm. You will find a sling a good solution, too, if your patient has a cut or bruised hand or wrist, which he must keep at rest until it begins to heal.

Whenever possible, use a triangular bandage to make a sling. Three large safety pins, however, can make an excellent emergency substitute.

You will need a very large triangular bandage to make your sling. As usual, muslin is a good choice.

Lay one end of the triangle over the patient's shoulder on his uninjured side, with the middle point of the triangle facing the injured arm. Let the other end hang straight, across his chest.

Gently, please, bend the patient's arm so that it is roughly parallel with his shoulders. Usually he will be more comfortable if his wrist is 4 or 5 inches higher than his elbow. Be very slow and careful as you bend his arm. Do not bend it farther if it causes him any pain, because pain is always a danger signal.

Now, with the arm and the triangle in position, carry the lower end of the triangle up over the patient's injured arm and shoulder. Tie the two ends at the back of his neck.

This leaves the point of the bandage at his elbow. Fold it over neatly and fasten it with a safety pin. Or you can twist the point until it is comfortably snug at the elbow, and tuck it into the bandage.

Be sure you leave the ends of your patient's fingers free to extend beyond the sling. By looking at his fingers, you can tell whether or not the circulation is cut off. If they turn pale or bluish, or if your patient complains that his fingers feel numb, the sling is much too tight.

Have you ever seen someone with his sleeve pinned across his coat front? This is one way to make a temporary arm sling.

ONE MORE WORD

By the time you can make even half of the bandages and slings we've talked about, you will be a great asset to your family's health. You have probably already made finger or elbow or knee bandages many times for yourself. Now, however, you'll have the satisfaction of making them the best way, with real nursing skill. Just one more word, and that word is— *practice!* It's fun to practice with your friends the way Gwen and Anne and I—in fact the entire Spencer Club—used to do at nursing school.

CHERRY ASKS

Have you practiced applying each type of bandage until you can now do each one quickly and neatly?

What kind of bandage would you use for a foot or hand wound?

Do you make your bandages snug, but not tight?

Can you name at least one injury in which you would use a cravat bandage? How do you make one?

What kind of bandage would you apply to an injured finger or toe?

Can you make a neat, comfortable sling?

~~~~~~

CHAPTER V

Never Delay First Aid

IF SOMEONE IS HURT AT YOUR HOUSE, THE SAFEST rule is to call the doctor immediately—without delay.

Delays are dangerous. If you wait, you give the injury or infection a chance to develop. Within a surprisingly short space of time, it can become really serious. Then it is several times harder for the doctor and your patient to effect a speedy recovery. But if you will let the doctor treat the injury or infection right away, he can often nip the condition in the bud.

Many times, as a hospital nurse, I've seen patients brought in with pneumonia or a serious infection. If only these people had consulted their doctors while their illness was still—or so they thought—"only a bad cold and chill" or "merely a scratch"!

Ask your own family doctor, and he will confirm the importance of *prompt* treatment.

Sometimes the doctor will be unable to come at once, or be unable to see you right away. You will have to give a simple treatment yourself, or help your mother give it.

If your mother isn't at home, you and your sister and brother will certainly want to know what to do. Your mother will probably be at home or nearby, though, and in that case you can be a great help to her.

Sometimes your mother may decide, on the basis of her experienced judgment, that the injury is not serious enough to call a doctor. Here are certain cases which you can recognize and treat at home:

CUTS

A cut is a wound—a break in the skin through which germs can enter the blood stream. Germs abound everywhere, and many can cause illness. Any break in the skin—a scratch, a scrape, a tear, a puncture—may be serious for this reason. No matter how small the wound—a pinprick which scarcely bleeds, or a slight scratch from your kitten—you should at once take steps against infection. Don't give germs a chance to get in and grow and cause trouble!

Suppose you and your mother are making sandwiches, and your mother cuts her finger a little on the bread knife. Perhaps you can do a better job of first aid than she can do for herself with one hand. How will you take care of the cut finger for her?

First of all, you will be careful not to touch the cut or the skin around it—even after you have washed your hands with soap and hot water, and dried them on a clean towel. You will be careful not to breathe on an open wound.

If the cut bleeds a little, wipe the edges clean with a sterile gauze dressing. Always wipe *away* from the wound. Do not disturb any blood clots that may form. Hold the dressing only by its corner. After wiping, discard the used dressing.

It is best not to attempt to clean the wound itself. *Do not* wash it with soap and water. *Do not* pour antiseptic into an open cut. Cleaning a wound is a job for the doctor.

All you have to do is apply an adhesive bandage or plastic strip. Of course the gauze part, not the adhesive, goes over the cut.

PUNCTURE WOUND

If it is a puncture wound—for instance a jab with an ice pick—the doctor should treat it at once! A puncture may lead to tetanus or lockjaw. Be especially alert if you happen to puncture yourself with a farm tool, since on farms horse manure is used as a fertilizer and that often carries tetanus germs. Another thing: since exploding fire crackers or pistol blanks can cause minute punctures in the skin, the doctor should see this type of wound at once.

Follow this procedure in case of a puncture wound, even a small one: First squeeze the wound at its edges so that it will bleed. Bleeding will carry off some of the germs and dirt. Second, apply a sterile dressing and a clean bandage. Third, go to the doctor promptly. He will give antitetanus toxin.

SCRATCHES

Sometimes a cut is only a tiny scratch. In that case your doctor may recommend applying a small amount of antiseptic to the cut and to the skin around it. Or he may prefer you to use no antiseptic, but wipe the scratch clean with boiled or fresh tap water. Either way, the aim—and your job as a first-aider—is to prevent any further germs from entering the cut. To treat your mother's hand, first apply a bandage.

BANDAGING A CUT

Apply a sterile gauze dressing or compress. Now, to hold it, put on a bandage, also of sterile gauze. Fasten the bandage firmly, preferably with adhesive tape—because if the dressing slips around on your mother's hand, it may touch an unsterile area and pick up germs. If the cut is quite small, an adhesive bandage or plastic strip may fit best.

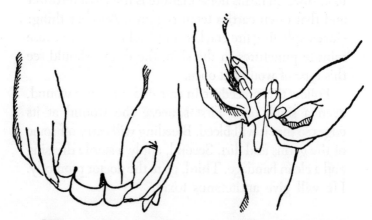

When applying an adhesive bandage, take hold of paper ends, which cover adhesive tape. Place dressing section over cut. Then peel back paper ends, securing adhesive firmly to skin's surface.

WATCH THE CUT

You and your mother will keep an eye on her cut finger to make sure it is healing properly. After a few hours you will want to look at it and apply a fresh, clean dressing. When you remove the old bandage and dressing, be careful not to tear the dressing from the wound, or it will bleed again. Be very gentle and slow about this.

Usually a minor cut will heal nicely. If you keep the wound clean and treat it correctly, infection won't set in. But if you are in any doubt, consult your doctor.

BLEEDING

One problem that you might face in treating a cut is the question of how to staunch bleeding. In deeper cuts, bleeding is always something you have to take care of. Severe bleeding can be as dangerous as infection. You do not want your patient to lose blood, because that will weaken him.

By the way, I take it for granted that you do not squeal and make silly faces at the sight of blood. Have you ever studied a drop or two of blood under a microscope at school? Perhaps you know that blood is composed of a fluid called plasma. It carries the red cells or corpuscles which supply your body with oxygen, and it carries the white corpuscles which fight back against germs.

A grown-up person who weighs 150 pounds has about four or five quarts (or eight to ten pints) of blood. Children have proportionately less. If a grown-up person loses two pints of blood (two cups) at once, or a child loses a proportionate amount, that is serious.

If someone is bleeding severely, do not take time to call a doctor. *You must stop the bleeding at once.* Every second counts. Your promptness and speed can save a life.

You have probably heard of tourniquets. But they are such a touchy subject that I mention them only to say—Don't!

As you probably know, a tourniquet is an extremely tight bandage, used only in the severest bleeding, and a dangerous device except in the most expert hands. It can lead to severe complications. So *don't* use a tourniquet.

The best way to stop bleeding in many cases is to put pressure on the bleeding place. Quickly remove any clothing that hides the wound. Take a clean handkerchief or whatever cloth or clothing is at hand —sterile is best, but don't delay to get it. Wad up the cloth, press it tightly against the wound, and hold it there firmly with your fingers. Keep on holding and pressing it there while the cut has a chance to clot and thus "cork up" the bleeding. That generally takes three to six minutes. If the cloth gets blood-soaked, do not take it away. Cover it with another dressing and keep on pressing *tightly* against the wound.

While you staunch the bleeding, keep your patient lying down, quiet and at rest. Loosen any tight cloth-ing. If it is his arm or leg which is bleeding, prop up the limb a little with a folded blanket or coat or whatever you have at hand. Do not handle or carry or walk your patient if you can avoid it. If you must move him, be very gentle. Don't talk to your patient any more than really necessary. A person who is bleeding severely is weak and frightened. Be calm and quiet yourself; that will help to calm him.

When the bleeding stops, you may very carefully and gently attempt to remove the wad of cloth. Caution!—if it sticks to the cut, so that pulling might start the bleeding again, leave it there for the doctor to remove. Just fasten it in place with a bandage. However, usually you can safely remove the wad of cloth and apply a sterile gauze dressing. Then apply a bandage. Here is where your triangular bandage and cravat bandage come in handy.

Of course have a doctor see the wound as promptly as possible. He can control any infection which may have set in.

In case a doctor cannot see your patient soon after you have stopped the bleeding, here are some things you can do to help him. Give the patient a drink of water, preferably warm—but not if he is unconscious or has a stomach injury. Don't give him any stimulants. If he is very pale, weak or clammy, or if he has bled very much, treat your patient for shock. Keep your patient warm and quiet until a doctor can treat him.

When you stop severe bleeding, you may very likely save a life. It is not hard to do. It takes speed, presence of mind, and a willingness to help another person.

Your job still is not finished. After someone has

had severe bleeding, you will want to make frequent checkups to make sure the bleeding (or hemorrhage) does not start again. If it does, you will give this same first aid again.

PRESSURE POINTS

Sometimes the bleeding comes in a steady flow. This means that a vein or smaller capillary is cut, and this is mostly the kind of bleeding we discussed just above. Sometimes, though, the bleeding comes in spurts and this means it comes from an artery. This bleeding is heavier and faster and quite serious.

The way you can control heavy, persistent bleeding is to apply pressure, at once, *firmly but gently*, with your hand or finger, at certain points.

Here is how this method works: When you press the artery against the bone, you decrease the blood flow. (Do *not* use a tourniquet, because it may crush and permanently injure the artery.) Pressure will not completely stop the bleeding, but will slow it down enough for you to apply a dressing firmly to the wound.

Never press very hard. Be gentle. Be careful.

Applying pressure is a good method to use also when your patient's hand or arm, or foot or leg, bleeds severely.

You can apply pressure at these six points where arteries lay:

1) If bleeding occurs in forearm or hand or fingers, press with your fingers on the inner side of the upper arm. The illustration shows you where. You can

feel the pulsing of the artery, even on your own arm. That is the exact spot to apply pressure. Press the artery *gently* and firmly against the bone of the arm.

2) If bleeding occurs in thigh, leg, foot or toe, place the palm of your hand against the middle of the groin. Here, again, if you feel for the pulsing of the artery, you will find the best spot to apply pressure.

3) If bleeding occurs from a wound of the neck, mouth, or throat, press with your fingers at the side of the throat. You can feel the artery pulsing at the side of the windpipe. Press *very gently* in the direction of the backbone. Pressure at the throat may make your patient unconscious. Use it with great caution and only as a last resort. Study the illustration, too.

4) If bleeding occurs

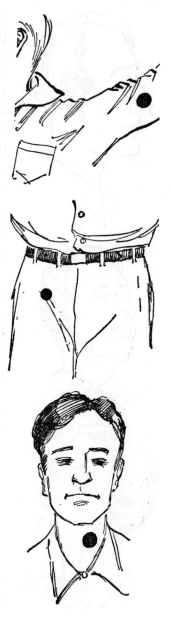

from a wound in the upper part of the head, feel for the artery just in front of the ear. Press this point with your fingers against the skull. Gradually increase the pressure of your fingers until the bleeding slackens enough for you to use a dressing.

5) If bleeding occurs from a facial wound below the eye and above the jawbone, the pressure point is at the jawbone, about an inch forward from the angle of the jaw. Place your fingers on the artery there and gradually increase your pressure until the bleeding comes under control. This pressure point does not apply to nosebleed, which we'll talk about later.

6) If bleeding occurs in the very uppermost part of the arm or the armpit or the shoulder, find the pulsing artery behind the inner end of the collarbone. Place your thumb there and press down, firmly, but

gently, in the direction of the first rib. Sometimes, if your patient is stocky and short-necked, this method will not work. If it doesn't, don't waste a second, but press your fingers directly at the area of the wound. Press at the *edges* of the wound.

Once you bring your patient's bleeding under control, then you will apply a dressing (sterile, if possible) and a bandage.

Of course you will have a doctor see your patient as quickly as possible.

INFECTED WOUNDS

Do I hear you object, "If I grab the nearest cloth to stop severe bleeding with, and it isn't sterile, won't I risk infection?" Yes, you will. But every second counts when your patient is bleeding heavily. Of course you will try to grab the nearest *clean* cloth. Even so, the wound may become infected.

And even in minor cuts, even when you treated your mother's cut finger correctly, there's a chance infection may still set in. That's why it's important for you to remove the dressing and look at your mother's finger every few hours, and also for several days after the accident.

Suppose that a day or two later, when you examine her finger, you find that the skin around the cut has grown red and tender. The finger looks swollen. Perhaps pus has formed. Your mother complains that the finger throbs. These are signs of infection. In other parts of the body, swollen glands—for instance, those at the sides of the throat—are also a sign of infection.

An infected cut, like any infection, is serious. Infected cuts are particularly serious on fingers or toes or at joints. First aid is not enough. *Always have a doctor treat infected cuts at once.* If you don't, a fever may develop and the infection can rapidly turn into a real illness.

Sometimes the doctor may not find it possible to see your patient at once. While you wait, persuade your patient to rest. In bed is best. (This lessens chances of spreading the infection throughout the entire system.)

A very hot saltwater solution, while you wait, which you apply with sterile gauze to the infected part, helps to soothe the soreness and reduce the swelling. If your patient can dip the infected finger or part into the hot solution, that is the best way. If not, you will use a freshly laundered towel, wring it out in the hot solution, and apply it repeatedly as a hot compress. Do this continuously for twenty minutes to an hour.

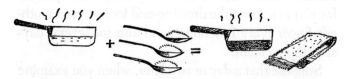

1 qt. boiling water   3 tbs. salt   1 qt. salt solution

This is how to make a sterile hot salt solution: you boil a quart of water and add about three heaping tablespoons of ordinary salt. Leave the solution in the same container in which you boiled it. Between applications, cover the solution to keep it clean. Re-heat it to as hot a temperature as is comfortable, before you apply it again.

These are only temporary measures, however. Be sure you call the doctor at once in case of any infected cut.

After the doctor treats the cut, he may decide it will heal better if left unbandaged and open to the air. Then, of course, you will follow the doctor's instruction.

NOSEBLEEDS

Most nosebleeds usually start from a physical cause. If you poke at your nose or bump it hard or fall on it, naturally your nose is going to object. A slight nosebleed is a minor matter. If you sit quietly with your head tilted back, the flow will often stop of its own accord.

When the nose bleeds severely, however, and for more than a few minutes—sometimes for an hour, if left unchecked—then you are confronted with a serious loss of blood. It's important to staunch the bleeding quickly. Here is how to do it:

Tell your patient to sit up (or prop him up) and hold his head slightly back. He must breathe through his mouth while you give the treatment. With your fingers, press the nostril on the bleeding side firmly against the center bone of the nose. If both of your patient's nostrils are bleeding, then press both nostrils firmly against the bone. Hold the pressure for several minutes, at least four or five minutes. This will allow a clot to form.

Now, when the bleeding lessens or stops, wring out a wash cloth in cold water. Place this cold compress over your patient's nose. If you have ice available, without leaving your patient for more than a minute or two, roll up a little ice in a towel. Or fill a small rubber bag (or a shower cap) with ice—only a little, so that it will not weigh heavily. Place this cold pack on your patient's nose.

Be sure to caution him not to blow his nose. Nor should he talk, cough, or walk around. If he does, the bleeding may start again. Keep him at rest.

An old-fashioned remedy, and still a good one, is to give your patient a little lemon juice to drink. It also helps to apply pressure to his upper lip. But you take these steps in addition to the first steps we discussed.

If the nosebleed persists and you find you cannot stop it within a few minutes, you had better call a doctor at once. Don't let the bleeding go on and on. A few, rare persons are "bleeders"—that is, their blood will not clot and only a physician's skill can save them. Probably your patient is not one of this rare type. Even so, stopping a really severe nosebleed is a job for a doctor.

While you are waiting for the doctor, you can take a narrow strip of sterile gauze and gently pack it into just the opening of the bleeding nostril. *Not* up into the nostril, and *not* in deeply. Leave an end of the gauze strip outside so the doctor can remove it easily.

CAREFUL WITH A SOILED DRESSING!

Because soiled dressings carry germs, you must be very particular to discard them properly. Doctors and nurses use forceps to lift off a soiled dressing. You'll find that good-sized tweezers make a perfectly good substitute. Lift off the soiled dressing with your tweezers and drop it into a paper bag. Close the bag firmly, and put it in the garbage can or, if you have a yard, burn it.

After you have used the tweezers, they are contaminated. Don't let the tweezers touch anything. If

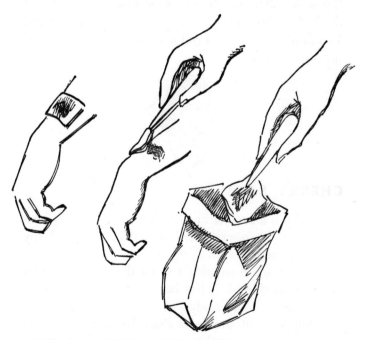

Whenever possible, remove soiled dressings to disposable paper bag with sterilized tweezers.

you have to set them down, put them on a piece of paper. You'll dispose of the piece of paper in a moment, holding it by one clean corner. Be sure you sterilize the tweezers by putting them for a few minutes into boiling water.

If you have no tweezers, use a square of newspaper, of several thicknesses to lift off the soiled dressing. Drop the paper and the dressing into a paper bag. Close the bag and dispose of it.

Once, as a very green student nurse, I was helping to remove a ward patient's soiled dressing and I handed Dr. Wylie the wrong forceps. Then I dropped the soiled dressing! So don't be discouraged if you don't do everything perfectly on your very first try. I couldn't either. But I did learn and in the end won my nurse's cap.

CHERRY SAYS

Why is a cut—or any break in the skin—a potentially serious matter? Is a small cut or scratch any less serious than a large one?

If you are in any doubt about the seriousness of a wound, or if it has become infected, call your doctor immediately.

Suppose your brother or sister develops a nosebleed when your mother is not at home? How would you stop the bleeding?

We now know that the two chief dangers in cuts
are 1) infection, and 2) bleeding. If your patient
is bleeding severely, first stop or lessen the flow.
Then take the necessary first aid measures, and
call a doctor.

What are the pressure points? (I admit this is a
hard question—but an important one. Read back
if you have to.)

A reminder: First aid is always temporary. It safe-
guards your patient *until the doctor can see him.*
All the treatments we are talking about are first-
aid measures only.

And remember: Every nurse and many wives and
mothers begin by learning the same techniques
you are now acquiring.

~~~~~~

CHAPTER VI

Bruises, Burns and Blisters

BRUISES

AT ONE TIME OR ANOTHER, WE'VE ALL MANAGED TO give ourselves a nasty bump. Bumps or bruises not only are highly unattractive, but sometimes are also extremely painful.

What exactly are bruises, you ask? They are closed wounds, injuries *underneath* the skin. What happens is that a blow or a fall breaks some of the tiny veins (capillaries) beneath the skin. Then blood spreads out into the tissues, and the skin quickly swells and turns reddish and sore. Later it turns a bluish hue and, as the bruise heals, brown or yellowish. Since bruises are the most common of all injuries, you probably have noticed these stages yourself.

You may decide that a bruise is too slight to need first aid. Usually a minor bruise will heal by itself.

However, in severe bruises, treatment is advisable. It helps to limit the swelling and discoloration, and it eases the soreness.

Dip a clean cloth, folded in several thicknesses, in very cold water. Apply it immediately to the bruised part. When this cold wet compress grows warm, in about three minutes, change it for a fresh, very cold wet cloth. If you have an ice bag, that is even better to use.

If you haven't a chance to treat the bruise until several hours after the injury, apply warm, wet cloths.

If your patient's (or your own) arm or leg is severely bruised, raise the limb slightly by propping it on a pillow. That will ease the pain.

When the skin is broken, give first aid as discussed for cuts.

Many bruises can be avoided. As our Superintendent of Nurses said about all injuries, the best treatment is to be a little careful and not get hurt in the first place.

BURNS

Have you ever seen someone so sunburned that his back and shoulders blistered?

Have you ever burned your finger on a match?

Have you ever read about people caught in a fire in a building, who needed hospital treatment for their burns?

Different as these situations are, they are all burns. If you touch a very hot pot handle, or a lighted match brushes your finger, that is a burn caused by heat contact. Electricity, and certain strong chemicals can cause contact burns, too. If steaming hot liquid splashes on your foot, that burn is called a scald.

All burns are painful and take a long time to heal. A burned hand or leg can keep you from your usual activities for weeks. A bad burn may disfigure the victim unless treated properly.

THREE DEGREES OF BURNS

You probably already know about the three degrees of burns. First-degree burns are small, mild injuries which redden but do not break the skin.

In second-degree burns, the skin blisters immediately or in several hours. In such cases you must watch for danger of infection.

In third-degree burns, the skin is cooked or charred, and deep tissues are destroyed. This is an extremely serious injury. A doctor should treat second- and third-degree burns at once.

With burns, you must deal with the serious dangers of shock and infection. Remember, shock and infection in extreme cases can cause death. Of course these are the cases where a doctor will be in charge. But there is a great deal you can do with your first aid. You can check shock in its early stages. You can prevent infection from ever starting.

If all this sounds awfully dire, it's because burns *are serious*. Did you know that burns and scalds cause more deaths among babies, small children, and old people than any other accident? You *can* take precautions to safeguard against anyone's getting burned.

TREATING SMALL FIRST-DEGREE BURNS

First-degree burns, where the skin is mildly reddened, can be surprisingly painful. You know for yourself how a burned finger can smart. For a superficial burn—for example if you barely touched that hot pot handle—run the burned finger under cool water. In case of a mild burn—if your small brother burned his hand on a match—apply sterile petrolatum ointment. Or use any other good burn ointment. Be sure your fingers and the applicator are clean. Now cover the burn with a sterile gauze dressing, and bandage. It's important to keep the burned area clean, because even in a first-degree burn there is danger of infection. A thick bandage, by keeping out air, will keep down the pain, too.

TREATING LARGE BURNS

An interesting fact is that when a small area of the body gets burned—a finger or hand—it is not nearly so serious an injury as when a *large* area is even mildly burned. If the burn on the patient's chest or back, for example, covers an extensive area, there is great danger of infection and shock. Have him lie down, with his head down. Keep him warm by covering him. Remove any loose, burned garments. Don't try to remove any clothing that sticks to the burned area. The doctor will do this. Your chief job is to keep your patient warm and at rest. Get an ambulance or car to take him to a hospital just as quickly as you can.

FOUR DON'TS

Don't apply cotton directly to a burn. It will stick.

Don't use boric acid or tea (tannic acid) in the burn solution. Use baking soda from your kitchen shelf. Or as a substitute, use Epsom salts.

Don't open blisters which form on the burned area. That is a job for the doctor. If they open by themselves, cover with a sterile dressing.

Don't put burn ointment on deep or wide burns.

AND TWO "DO'S"

Your patient in shock might appreciate a few sips of water. Give them to him at frequent intervals. (Of course you must not give a drink of water, or anything else to swallow, to any patient who is unconscious.)

Call the doctor or an ambulance at once whenever someone is extensively burned. Burn cases can't wait.

HOW TO SOOTHE A SEVERE BURN

If you are waiting at home for the car or ambulance to come, here is what you can do for the burn: Make

1 qt. warm water + 3 tbs. baking soda = 1 qt. burn solution

a solution of one quart of warm tap water and three tablespoonsful of baking soda. If you don't have baking soda, Epsom salts will do, in the same amount. Tear clean white sheeting or muslin into compresses. Dip these in the warm solution, and apply to the burned area. Wrap dry towels around the compresses. Doing this will ease the pain, and also provide a measure of cleanliness. Remember, keep your patient covered and lying down.

A TRUE STORY

My first serious burn case came to Spencer Hospital when I was a student nurse there. He was seven years old and his nickname was Winky. A hot-water boiler at Winky's house had exploded in his face, leaving him with a third-degree burn. We hospital people had to see to it that the tissues of his face healed, and then the little boy was to have plastic surgery.

Because I was working on Emergency Ward the morning Winky's father brought him in, I was one of those who helped the doctor give Winky his first emergency treatment. You can imagine how concerned I was to do the best possible job. I found that a big part of my job was to reassure Winky. Like anyone who is badly injured, he was frightened. Besides, Winky had no mother, and his father kept saying foolish, upsetting things like, "He'll be disfigured! No one will want to look at him." It took a lot of work to convince Winky, and eventually his father, that with good hospital care he would come out as good as new.

Not all burns are as serious as Winky's was. However, as a good first-aider you will want to take good care of *any* burn.

BURNS FROM CHEMICALS

In case a strong acid or alkali or other chemical splashes on you or your patient, wash it off at once with clean water. Tap water will do nicely. Use lots of water and wash continuously until you feel sure you have washed all the chemical away. Then, if there is any sign of a burn, you may apply a burn ointment. If you decide the burn requires it, apply a sterile dressing, spread with petrolatum.

If any chemical splashes into the eye, be careful and be quick. Wash out the eye immediately, over and over again, with a great deal of clean water. To do this, have your patient lie down. Then carefully pour cupful after cupful of water into the inner corner of his eye. If lime or an alkali has splashed into the eye, use milk. Keep washing out the eye until you are satisfied that you have washed all the chemical away. Then, if you have some clean olive oil or mineral oil or castor oil, put a few drops into the eye and cover with a sterile gauze. Then, even though the eye may *seem* to be perfectly all right, it is essential to consult a doctor.

SUNBURN

"It's only sunburn," so many people say. They do not realize that a severe sunburn can be a serious *burn*.

Or they will say, "The sun wasn't out, so I couldn't

be very badly sunburned." But on cloudy or hazy days, the sun's rays are filtered through the clouds and may actually be stronger than on a sunny day. Even strong reflections of the sun's rays from a lake or on the sandy beach or, in winter, reflected from a big snowbank can cause a burn if you are exposed to them.

SUNTAN, NOT SUNBURN

You can protect yourself by gradually exposing yourself to the sun for just a few minutes each day, at first. Start with fifteen minutes, or less. After you have acquired a tan, then it is safe to stay in the sun for longer periods. Even so, you'll be wise to apply cocoa butter or a good oil or burn ointment right away when you come into strong sunshine. Some people use vinegar with good results. When you come out of the water after swimming, put on a robe for a few minutes until your skin dries off—this will help prevent a bad burn.

These measures help, but they don't guarantee that you won't get badly sunburned. The wise thing to do is not to stay in the sun too long at a stretch. Especially you blondes and redheads. If you are very fair-skinned and unable to tan, you'll *have* to take the sun in small doses—unless you want to turn as red as a boiled lobster.

TREATING SUNBURN

Most sunburns are first or second degree burns. In less severe sunburns, you'll find mild redness, dryness, and some peeling or scabbing. Apply calamine lotion. It is soothing and will not stain your clothes. Olive oil and petrolatum are good, too. There are also several excellent commercial burn ointments which your druggist can recommend.

With a more severe sunburn, you will be confronted with considerable redness of the skin, tenderness or soreness, itching, and after a while, blistering and peeling. This needs good care on your part. If the blistering covers a large area, coat a sterile gauze dressing with petrolatum, and apply the dressing to the blistered part. *Don't* break or open the blisters.

Careful! Is there a good deal of blistering? Or does the burn cover quite a large area? Are you, or is your patient, running a fever? Is there a chill? Or headache or swelling, or any other sign of illness? If you notice *any* of these symptoms, consult a doctor promptly.

BLISTERS

Now let's talk about blisters which are *not* caused by sunburn. They are usually caused by some sort of chafing, friction, or pressure. An ill-fitting shoe rubbing against your heel, for instance, will do the nasty trick.

But it's just as easy to raise a blister by using tools without gloves or some sort of cloth between you and the rake or sandpaper to cut down on friction. You'll need gloves or some sort of hand protection, too, for a fast game of tennis or a round of archery. And when working in the kitchen, remember that a potholder is a must for handling hot utensils.

My young friend, Midge Fortune, describes blisters as "a big nuisance." Her father, Dr. Fortune, says yes, but that definition is hardly medically correct. A blister is a slightly raised area of skin, filled with a watery fluid.

The best thing you can do about blisters is to leave them alone. Gently wash the blister and the skin around it with soap and water, and cover loosely with a sterile dressing. This will keep the area clean and help prevent further chafing.

Often the blister will dry out and disappear.

Don't open a blister! Such tampering can lead to serious infection. Opening a blister is a job for the doctor.

If the blister bursts and opens of its own accord, treat it as you would any other open wound. Remember, this does *not* apply to burn and sunburn blisters. Keep the opened place clean by washing it with soap and warm water. Or use an antiseptic around the *edges* of the open blister. Dry the area with sterile gauze and cover it with a sterile gauze compress.

Blisters, especially those rubbed on your foot, can be surprisingly dangerous. It's always a good idea to have your doctor see the wound.

CHERRY SAYS

Do you know how best to treat a bruise?

Were you ever sunburned? How did it happen? What is the safest way to acquire a suntan?

Can you describe a first-degree burn? And what are the symptoms of a second-degree burn? (I just hope you never encounter a third-degree burn. But it's wise to know how to give first aid for this most serious of burns.

If you burned your finger ever so slightly on a hot pan or match flame, what would you do to soothe the smarting?

Remember, use burn ointment only when the skin is mildly reddened—never for deep or wide burns.

If someone is splashed with a chemical which burns him, wash off the chemical with quantities of tap water.

What can cause blisters besides burns? How do you keep a blister clean?

~~~~~~

CHAPTER VII

Coping with the World Outdoors

IT'S WONDERFUL TO GET OUTDOORS. PICNICS, HIKES, camp trips—we look forward to them all with a good deal of excitement. But there are potential mishaps along the trail which we should know how to avoid and, when we do bump into them, how to treat. Let's take a look at them.

POISON IVY

Three plants to avoid—because they can cause a skin rash—are poison ivy, poison oak, and poison sumac.

Look at the pictures and you'll learn to recognize each leaf. Poison ivy is a shiny low shrub, bright-colored in the fall. Sometimes it grows along the ground or hugs a fence or climbs a tree or pole.

Poison oak is a shiny vine. It, too, turns a bright color in the autumn. Poison sumac, on the other hand, is a low bush or tree, green all summer, orange in spring and fall.

Poison oak (climber)   Poison sumac   Poison ivy

A good rule to follow when you're out in the woods is not to touch any leaves. Danger signals are three-leaf clusters and white berries.

On a lively hike with friends it's easy to stumble, chase, or be chased into a patch of any of these plants. But if you have ever itched and blistered from their rash, you know it's worthwhile to watch for and to avoid these plants.

The plant secretes an oil which, in even the tiniest amount, poisons the skin. Just brushing against a poisonous leaf may be enough to cause a rash. Some people are affected by the small amounts of oil carried by insects, by a shoe, or by smoke when these leaves are burned. Occasionally you can catch poison ivy from someone who already has it. When you are perspiring heavily, your skin is more susceptible to any of these three poisonous plants.

In case you come into contact with poison ivy, in any of these ways, you may see the results at once, or you may not notice anything for as long as nine days. (A very few people are immune, but immunity does not always last.) Your skin will grow red and itchy. Small blisters may develop. In a severe case, the poisoned part may swell up alarmingly. This calls for a doctor's treatment.

As soon as you know that you have been exposed to one of these three poisonous plants, here is what you should do:

First, don't touch other, uncontaminated parts. Don't scratch, because that will invite infection.

Make a heavy soap lather—strong laundry soap is preferable. Use the lather and warm water to wash the poisoned part. Don't rub, don't use a brush or rough cloth. Don't let the lather touch other parts of your skin. Lathering five or six times helps to check the inflammation. Then wash thoroughly with rubbing alcohol. Rinse with clear water, and dry.

If you have a really bad case, make a thick soap paste and leave it on overnight. Always consult a doctor as soon as possible.

Calamine lotion is a good thing to use after the soap lather and rubbing alcohol. If you go to camp or go on a hike, take calamine lotion with you. You should also always keep a supply in your first-aid kit.

HIVES

When I was growing up, there was always at least one boy or girl in my class who persistently had hives. No matter what the rest of us ate at picnics or parties, that one unhappy person broke out with a pink, itchy rash. Sometimes it was strawberries he could not eat (and could not leave alone); sometimes it was shellfish. Or sometimes it was the aspirin he took later.

There are two things you can do about hives. First, track down the offending food or foods, and—next time it is offered—say, "No, thank you." Second, apply calamine lotion. One good substitute is a strong baking soda solution. To make this use three teaspoons baking soda to one glass of cold water.

As usual, you would be sensible to see your doctor. Hives don't last more than one or two days at a time, but the itching and unsightliness are as unpleasant as any other form of allergy.

BITES

If we had the heavy hide of a rhinoceros, or the armor plate of an armadillo, instead of our unprotected skin, we human beings would not be so vulnerable to bites from animals and insects. As it is, we can be harmed and we need to know how to take care of ourselves. Fortunately the medical sciences have discovered and developed wonderful techniques. The main job is up to you—to know these techniques, and use them promptly and exactly.

INSECT BITES

Let's start with the smallest attackers. Many insects are useful and beneficial to human beings. But a few, like certain ticks, are carriers of disease. Even without carrying disease, bites and stings can cause soreness and swelling—as you know from a bee sting—or inflammation.

Don't scratch! Scratching can cause infection.

If the insect or its "sting" remains on or in the skin, remove it. Take it from below without squeezing it. Now apply cold water or cold ammonia water, to ease any pain. To relieve itching, make a paste of baking soda and cold cream and apply that. For itchy mosquito and chigger bites, calamine lotion is soothing.

If you have been bitten by a wood tick (see illustration), consult your doctor. These ticks often carry Rocky Mountain spotted fever.

Female tick (enlarged)   Male tick (enlarged)

DOG BITES

Do you have a dog? Or are you acquainted with some of the dogs in your neighborhood? They probably are friendly and hardly ever nip anyone. But now and then a dog *may* bite—a cat may, too. Since the animal's teeth and mouth carry a great many germs, the person bitten will be in risk of infection.

Animal bites on the head and face are particularly dangerous.

RABID DOGS

A special danger in dog bites is rabies. (This is also called hydrophobia.) Rabies can make a person dangerously ill. You can recognize a "rabid" or "mad" dog by these signs: It is very excited, it darts about, it may stagger as if it has a broken back, or be unable to close its mouth. A dog which runs wild and froths at the mouth is not necessarily rabid; he probably has fits. But any animal bite is risky.

Don't make the mistake of killing the animal, unless there is absolutely no other way to protect the people around. Destroying the animal makes it nearly impossible for the laboratory people to discover and advise the doctor whether or not the dog actually has rabies.

WHAT TO DO ABOUT A RABID DOG

The best thing to do, and also the most humane thing for the dog, is to ask the police to catch it, if possible, and turn it over to a veterinarian.

You can protect your entire community if you will notify your local health authorities, or your police, about the bite and the dog which shows signs of rabies.

Sometimes, though, a dog may have rabies and not appear sick at all. That is why in *any* case of dog bite—whether it's a playful nip from Fido or a bite from a stray—you'll need to take the following prompt first-aid measures.

FIRST AID FOR DOG BITES

Wash the wound thoroughly in water. Running water from a faucet will remove the saliva. Don't rub, but with a sterile gauze compress, wash the wound with soap and water. Rinse, and apply an antiseptic (mild iodine is good). Then put on a sterile dressing and bandage. *Have a doctor treat the victim at once.*

The doctor may decide to give a vaccination called the Pasteur treatment. This immunizing must be done immediately. If there is a delay and the victim develops symptoms of rabies, it will be too late to cure him. But with promptness, the disease can be prevented.

SNAKE BITES

My twin brother, Charlie, when we were both ten years old, kept a harmless little garter snake as a pet. Our mother was not enthusiastic about meeting even a small snake in Charlie's room, and we moved it to a flower bed beside our garage. I never objected to Charlie's pet, because all living creatures are interesting. If you've noticed, many snakes have beautiful colors and markings, and most of them are harmless.

SNAKES TO AVOID

However, four kinds of our North American snakes are poisonous. If you are outdoors in the country a good deal, you may have seen them. It's a good idea to be able to recognize them, so that you can keep out of their way. Snakes usually will not strike except in self-defense. They will quietly move away, as a rule, unless you come too close to them. Certainly you won't want to provoke a rattlesnake, a moccasin, a copperhead, or a coral snake.

All of these, except the coral snake, are called pit-vipers, because of a small, deep pit between the snake's nostril and eye on each side of its head. The pits look like a second set of nostrils. Pit-vipers have thick bodies, tapering at either end, and grow quite large. If you see such a snake, or even a picture of one, you'll know this is a poisonous snake. It carries poison in its sharp fangs, or teeth, which swing forward like a flash when the snake strikes. These poisons are called venom, and in emergencies you must keep your head and give speedy first aid.

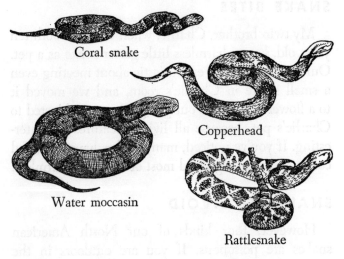

Coral snake

Copperhead

Water moccasin

Rattlesnake

WHERE TO BE WATCHFUL

How can you avoid these snakes? One way is by knowing where they are. You can find the rattlesnake, which is the commonest pit-viper, in twenty-six different sizes and markings throughout many areas of the United States. The copperhead lives in the eastern and south central parts of our country. If you're anywhere from Virginia to the Rio Grande, and near water or swamps, this is the home of the cottonmouth moccasin.

Coral snakes, the fourth kind, are small. They are marked with broad, brilliant bands of red and black separated by narrow bands of yellow. They do not strike; they bite and hang on, leaving deceptively small fang marks. But they usually will not bite if you do not provoke them. You'll find coral snakes in the southernmost states, from California to Florida.

HOW TO PROTECT YOURSELF

It's not likely that you will come anywhere near any of these snakes. Even if you do, if you are reasonably cautious about not walking blindly into undergrowth, you can keep out of their way. Look before you take each step, particularly at the edges of a path. Look before you reach out to pick berries or flowers, or reach up to grasp a rocky ledge. A snake may feel you are intruding on his resting place. Heavy, high shoes or boots, and leather gloves or gauntlets are a good protection in certain places. Besides, local people will warn you what places to stay away from. You'd best listen to them!

HARMLESS SNAKE BITES

In case of a bite by a harmless snake, you need not be alarmed. Of course you will promptly take the same steps as you would with any other wound. Apply a sterile dressing and bandage, and consult a doctor.

It's reassuring to know that eighty-five per cent of those persons bitten by poisonous snakes get well, even without any treatment. But since no one wants to belong to the other fifteen per cent, it's best to know the treatment for poisonous snake bite.

You must administer treatment as speedily as you possibly can. Poison acts fast.

POISONOUS SNAKE BITES

First, and very important, make your patient lie down immediately and keep quiet. If he moves around, the poison will spread throughout his body.

Quickly wrap or tie a firm band around the limb, about an inch or two above the bite. Use anything you have at hand—a stocking, a scarf, a belt, handkerchief, bandage. Tie it moderately tight. Try to place the injured limb lower than the rest of the body.

Now sterilize a knife or razor blade in a flame or in iodine or alcohol. If you haven't anything to sterilize with, go ahead anyway in this one case. Make small cross-shaped cuts, ¼- to ⅜-inch deep, through the fang marks. Be careful to avoid veins and tendons; you can see these just under the surface of the skin.

Once the cuts are made, your job is to remove the poison by suction. If you have a suction cup with a rubber bulb, that is best. Or take a bottle or small-mouthed jar, heat it in hot water or by burning paper or cotton inside it. Immediately apply the mouth of the bottle over the cross-cuts. As the bottle cools, suction will take place.

Suppose you have none of these things right at hand. Then you should suck on the wound by mouth, and spit out the fluid. It will not harm you, even if you swallow some. Venom is dangerous in the blood stream but is destroyed in the stomach. Rinse your mouth with clear water.

Last and important, send for a doctor as quickly as possible. The doctor will give antivenin serum.

Both speedy first aid and antivenim serum are necessary.

If your patient seems cold or sweaty or exhausted, give hot black coffee or tea or hot water to combat shock.

Don't cover the bitten area.

MORALE COUNTS

Did you know that some people have actually died of fright, when bitten by a non-poisonous snake? It's very important for you to reassure your patient, and keep him in good spirits. This is so in any illness, but especially true in this case.

STEPPING ON A RUSTY NAIL

You remember that earlier we talked about puncture wounds, and how tricky they can be. One kind you'll want to be particularly careful about occurs when someone steps on a rusty nail. Or if someone jabs himself with a rusty icepick or rusty scissors or rusty pitchfork, be alert.

Rust is dragged deep into the wound, and will

almost certainly cause infection. A real possibility is blood poisoning, which can be fatal. This can be avoided if you will have a physician see the wound at once. He will clean it out and give antitetanus toxin. Until he can see your patient, it helps a little to squeeze *gently* around the edges of the wound. This will encourage bleeding and get rid of some of the poison. But most important—

Don't delay getting medical help.

SPLINTERS

Wood splinters cause the smallest of skin wounds, but don't ignore a splinter. If you let one remain in your finger, you invite infection and swelling. Sometimes, too, a splinter carries dirt with it under the skin. Remove the splinter right away.

HOW TO REMOVE A SPLINTER

First, apply an antiseptic to the skin. Then sterilize a fine needle, or tweezers, by holding it for a few moments in a match flame. Don't touch or blow on the clean point while it cools. Now, with the sterile needle or tweezers, gently remove the splinter. Once it is out, a little pressure to encourage bleeding will wash the wound from inside out. Last, apply a sterile dressing or small compress.

IF A SPLINTER WON'T COME OUT

If you find you can't remove the splinter, or if it is a splinter of glass or metal, have the doctor take it out.

Really go to the doctor for a small matter like a balky splinter? Yes, because even a small wound can have large consequences.

It's like the riddle: When do 2 and 2 make more than 4? When they make 22. You never can tell in advance what an injury is going to add up to. But the medical sciences have given us fine techniques for getting well and keeping well. Let's use them.

CHERRY SAYS

How can you recognize poison ivy? Do poison oak and poison sumac look similar to poison ivy?

The best way to treat poison ivy, oak or sumac rash is to wash the part continuously with a thick soap lather. Then wash with rubbing alcohol, rinse and dry.

Can a food or medicine which disagrees with you cause the pink, itchy rash called hives?

Calamine lotion is soothing for hives. So is our friend, baking soda solution.

Calamine lotion is good, too, for mosquito and chigger bites. But what would you apply for insect and bee stings?

> If itchy, don't scratchy,
> Your skin will be patchy.
> (Contributed by Gwen Jones)

You can help your entire community if you will re-

port to your police department or local health
authorities the presence of a dog which you be-
lieve has rabies.

How does a rabid or "mad" dog behave? Does he
necessarily froth at the mouth?

Why must you not delay a second in giving first aid
for poisonous snake bite?

Is stepping on a rusty nail a serious injury? Why?

Be sure, when you remove a splinter, to sterilize the
needle in a flame first.

~~~~~~

CHAPTER VIII

Shock and Unconscious-ness

SHOCK

HAVE YOU NOTICED HOW OFTEN WE'VE MENTIONED shock in the chapters up till now? That's because shock generally occurs along with any serious injury. Much loss of blood can cause shock, too. So can bad burns. So can poisoning. Once in a while shock happens when someone is faced by sudden bad news—or sudden good news!—or undergoes any other great emotional stress.

Do you know what shock is? It is a depressed condition in which the blood vessels in the abdomen fail to do their circulatory work properly, and as a result your patient's brain and heart fail to receive a sufficient blood supply.

Shock may be slight; you know the weak, empty feeling you have when you cut or smash your finger. Or shock may lead to complete collapse and death, in extreme cases. Sometimes being in shock is more serious than the injury itself. It may not appear for some minutes or hours.

You can help greatly by *preventing* shock before it ever appears. Give immediate first aid for shock if these symptoms appear:

HOW TO RECOGNIZE SHOCK

Your patient will be pale and cold. The skin of his hands and face will feel cooler than normal; he may shiver. Sometimes perspiration will break out on his forehead or around his mouth. He may feel nauseated or want to throw up. His breathing will be shallow and irregular, his pulse fast and weak. He will be extremely weak. He may be confused, frightened, or nervous.

FIRST AID FOR SHOCK

Whether or not these symptoms appear, give immediate first aid for shock to any injured person.
Do not move your patient.

Have him lie down at once, with his head lower than his body, if you can, or at least level with body. But if he finds it hard to breathe, supply a pillow. Raise his feet a few inches. (Exceptions to this rule are: nosebleed, chest injury, head injury.)

Keep him warm and quiet. Gently place a blanket or coat under him. Cover him lightly, and reassure him with a few words.

While you want to keep your patient warm, do not overheat him. If you lack covers and must use a hot water bottle, test it against your own wrist to make sure it is just moderately warm. You see, a person in shock can be easily burned. Place the hot water bottle at his feet, or, if you don't fill it too full so that it won't be heavy, place it on his abdomen.

GIVE THESE STIMULANTS FOR SHOCK

Stimulants are much less important than the above steps; they only help to keep the patient warm.

If the doctor is going to see your patient very soon, give him nothing to drink. But if you must count on a wait of an hour or more, you may give him sips of comfortably hot water, or hot coffee, tea, broth, or milk. Or you may give warm shock solution. This is made by stirring 1 teaspoon ordinary table salt and ½ teaspoon baking soda into 1 quart of water. (A quart is four cupfuls.)

Don't give more than a cupful of liquid at a time; a few teaspoonfuls may be enough. Hold the teaspoon or cup for your patient, and gently support his head. *Exception:* Never give fluids to a person who is unconscious, vomiting, or to someone with an abdominal injury.

If you cannot bring your patient back to a normal condition within several minutes, call a doctor at once to combat shock.

BE GENTLE, BE REASSURING

The less you handle and talk to your patient in shock, the better. Don't try to move him. Don't ask questions unless really necessary. Be as gentle and quiet as you can, while keeping him warm and at rest and giving any other needed first aid. And remember, your patient needs your encouragement.

Besides shock there are several other ways a person can lose consciousness.

UNCONSCIOUSNESS

I don't mean simply fainting for joy—or getting knocked out in a prize fight—or seeing stars after a terrific bump on the head. These are perfectly good ways to "go out like a light," of course.

But there are many causes. For example, *accidents* such as an automobile crash, or a fall, or a severe blow on the head can cause a person to lose consciousness. (If the blow on the head causes an injury to the brain, that is called a concussion.) There are certain *illnesses*—stroke in older people, heart attack, taking poison, excessive drinking of alcohol, severe bleeding, diabetes, and many other illnesses—which can cause unconsciousness. There are *injuries* to consider: simple fainting, sunstroke, heat exhaustion, drowning, and others which we'll talk about.

DANGER SIGNAL

Unconsciousness is a danger signal exactly because it can be caused by so many different illnesses or accidents or emergencies. It is a signal to you as a first-aider that something is seriously wrong. Only a doctor can diagnose what that something is.

Send for a doctor quickly. Give first aid to bring the patient back to consciousness.

HOW TO RECOGNIZE UNCONSCIOUSNESS

How can you tell when a person is unconscious? He seems to be asleep or in a faint. He may have stopped, or almost stopped, breathing. He may give incoherent replies and mumble, if partially unconscious—or he may be silent and completely unconscious. Finally, his face is not quite its normal color.

The hue of his face provides you with useful clues. You can remember to look for red, white, or blue, the colors of our flag. When the patient's face has a tinge of one of those colors, it tells you these things:

WHAT TO DO

1) *Red unconsciousness,* or a flushed face. Blood is congested in the head and face. It is a signal that the patient has had a stroke, or apoplexy, or a skull fracture, or other head injury. *What to do:* Keep him lying down and quiet. Raise his head and shoulders slightly. Loosen any tight collar or tie or scarf. Apply cold compress or ice bag to his head. Keep him just moderately warm. Give no stimulants. Artificial respiration will *not* help. Call a doctor.

2) *White unconsciousness.* The patient's face is pale, his pulse weak. These are symptoms of shock or fainting or severe bleeding. *What to do:* Keep the patient lying down and quiet. Place his head lower than

his body (a pillow under the hips does this), or at least have his head level with his body. Keep him warm, but not sweating. Give no stimulants. Call a doctor.

3) *Blue unconsciousness.* The patient's face has a slight bluish tinge, his pulse and breathing are weak or have stopped. This is a signal of drowning or suffocation or heart attack. *What to do:* Be quick if you want to save a life! Send someone to call a doctor at once. Keep the patient lying down and quiet. Start artificial respiration at once if he is not breathing. (See Artificial Respiration on page 110.) Keep the patient warm with blankets, coats, or a windbreaker.

Call a doctor promptly in every case.

PLEASE DON'T

Remember, you can't arouse an unconscious person by shaking him, nor shouting at him, nor by splashing cold water on him. Let him lie quietly while you summon a doctor. You *can* bring a person back to consciousness, and normal color and breathing, by giving good first aid. Being quiet is important.

DETECTIVE WORK

You may have to do some detective work in order to discover the cause of the person's unconsciousness. Also, you'll need to learn *all* the facts in order to give a helpful report to the doctor.

You see, unconsciousness is tricky to trace back to its cause. Suppose an elderly person has fallen in his room. It may look as if he stumbled, fell against the radiator, and in falling suffered a head injury. Actually, though, he may have had a stroke. Or he may accidentally have swallowed poison.

It's your job, as an alert first-aider, to look around for such things as poison bottles, escaping gas, or a live electric wire (careful!). Outdoors, look for any signs of a hit-and-run automobile accident.

Look, too, for head injury or bleeding. Look to see whether the pupils of his eyes are of different size—and report all these symptoms to the doctor.

Your alertness and your calm, quiet first aid can be of the greatest help.

Now, because unconsciousness occurs in different ways and requires different treatment, let's discuss the most common kinds.

WHY PEOPLE FAINT

Mostly people faint if they have gone without food for a very long time. Or if they stay in a crowded room where there isn't enough air to breathe. Or if they are in acute pain. Or if they are overtired, and especially if they are standing. A few persons feel "gone" at the sight of blood, although most of us are able to control this reaction. Once in a while, some emotional shock or fear (for instance, of a treatment) may cause fainting.

HOW YOU CAN PREVENT FAINTING

If you see someone turn pale and weak and perspiration breaks out on his forehead—or if you see that he is injured—quickly assist him or her to lie down. Don't let him faint and fall! He could hurt himself more badly by falling than by fainting.

FIRST AID FOR FAINTING

Have your patient lie down flat. If you yourself feel faint and your vision blurs, lie down until the feeling passes. Lying down flat, or with the head slightly lower than the body, brings back a sufficient blood supply to the brain.

If lying down can't be managed, bend your patient forward at the waist so that his head is on a lower level than his heart. Loosen any tight clothing.

If he says he can swallow, offer him a drink of water, or tea or coffee. Keep your patient lying down until you are sure he has really recovered.

If these measures do not work quite quickly, cover your patient and call a doctor. As a rule most persons recover rapidly upon lying down.

ELECTRIC SHOCK

As you know, electric shock can cause a person to lose consciousness. First, be sure your hands are dry and be careful not to touch any wires yourself. Don't touch the victim if a wire touches him. Avoid any grounded objects (that is, objects which directly, or by pipes, touch the ground—for example, a sink or bathtub). Remove the victim from contact with the wire *only by encircling the wire with a DRY towel or sheet,* and pulling the wire away from him. Don't touch the wire. (Please consult Chapter XII for more about what you should do in accident prevention and rescues.) Call a doctor. And if there are loose wires, or especially if the accident occurs in a bathroom, call the electric company for help.

MIDGE NEARLY ELECTROCUTES HERSELF

One dark, rainy afternoon when I was visiting at home between nursing jobs, my young friend Midge Fortune came over to bake brownies with me. We were just putting the pans of batter in the oven when the light over the worktable, next to the sink, blinked and went out. I was busy adjusting the oven heat and didn't notice what Midge was up to. If I'd turned around ten seconds later, Midge would have already joined the angels. Ever helpful, and not thinking, she had climbed into the wet sink in her stocking feet and was just reaching up to unscrew the worn-out light bulb. I shouted at Midge so loudly that the Martins next door came running. Fortunately none of us had to give Midge first aid—only a lecture and a small scolding. (Midge has never cared much for brownies since that day.)

FIRST AID FOR ELECTRIC SHOCK

First be sure you observe the safety measures in the paragraph above entitled "Electric Shock." Then give the victim artificial respiration (page 110) at once.

Keep it up until your patient is breathing regularly and easily of his own accord, or until the doctor can take charge. Sometimes after electric shock, it may take several hours of artificial respiration to bring the patient back to consciousness. The effort *can* be successful. You would need other people to relieve you and take turns with you, of course.

HEART EMERGENCIES

It's not very likely that you will be called upon to help in case of a heart attack. But this is a common emergency among older people, and it never hurts to have information.

First of all, don't panic. Some people, if they have *any* pain about the heart or chest, take fright unnecessarily. It may be indigestion, or pleurisy, or a warning of pneumonia. Besides, not all heart flutters are serious.

HOW TO RECOGNIZE HEART ATTACK

Three separate types of symptoms will tell you whether this is heart attack:

1. In one kind of heart emergency, the person shows the same signs as in fainting—face pale, the pulse weak, sometimes chest pain, sometimes loss of consciousness.

2. In the second type, the patient has great pain in the heart region. He is often very frightened. He may or may not lose consciousness.

3. In the third type, his face may be red and he

cannot breathe lying down. He *must* sit up, even if you have to prop him up, and sometimes help him lean forward. He remains conscious.

FIRST AID FOR HEART ATTACK

You must keep your patient absolutely quiet. In the first two groups, have him lie down. In the third case, prop up your patient to sitting position.

Cover your patient lightly, just enough to keep him warm.

Call a doctor at once.

Don't let your patient exert himself in the slightest way. Keep him absolutely still. Keep his surroundings as quiet and peaceful as you possibly can.

Look in your patient's pockets or handbag. He may carry medicine for just such an emergency. Read the instructions on the package carefully, and place one tablet under his tongue—gently, please.

One of the most important things you can do is to give your patient courage. He's frightened, and this makes his illness worse. It's up to you to be calm and confident, and to reassure him.

HEART ATTACKS MAY BE MINOR

When I was a department store nurse, during the Christmas shopping season, an older woman who had a heart condition was brought into the infirmary. She had fainted for a few moments, and a floor supervisor brought her up to me in a wheel chair. She was able to tell me her son's name and office telephone number, so that I could call him to have him take her home. Of course I had her lie down on one of the cots and rest for an hour first.

Now, notice two interesting things: This woman was aware she had a heart condition, was under a physician's care, and was able to tell me what I needed to know as I checked her over. Thus I found out the second thing—that her fainting spell was due to the crowds and close air and excitement. Though she had come close to a heart attack, she had not actually suffered one—or else it was a very minor one.

After an hour's bed rest, and then a bracing cup of hot tea, this woman was quite well enough to go home under her son's escort. I did emphasize her need for more rest when she reached home, and recommended calling her doctor.

EPILEPTIC CONVULSIONS

Many people are frightened by the name and symptoms of this illness. Of course that is an unnecessary and not very intelligent way to behave. An epileptic person who is subject to sudden loss of consciousness and sudden attack of illness needs prompt help. It is not at all difficult to help him, and a bystander who knows how can do a real service.

Here is an illness in which the patient falls unconscious to the floor, thrashes about, and may hurt himself by thrashing against something. He may bite his tongue accidentally. Or he may partly swallow his tongue, and choke.

HOW TO HELP

You can't stop the thrashing movements and shouldn't try. You can gently help him to move away from any dangerous object, such as moving machinery. You *can* wrap a pencil in cloth, or fold a handkerchief into a long, bulky strip, and place this between the patient's teeth. This gag will restrain him from biting or swallowing his tongue. Put a pillow or folded coat under his head to protect it.

The convulsion probably will subside in a few minutes. Afterwards, the patient will seem drowsy and forgetful. Or he may drift into unconsciousness. Let him sleep. Don't disturb him with any questions. With rest, he will feel well and his usual self again.

AN EMERGENCY AT SCHOOL

I remember when I was in the third grade in school that one child in our class had "the falling sickness." We had a wise, kind teacher who explained to us that a convulsion was nothing to be afraid of, and that no one should be mean enough to tease this child when he woke up. And the teacher used the handkerchief-pencil device which I've described.

As a matter of fact, no one in our class was disturbed. It was my earliest lesson on how to keep calm in the face of an emergency. That child was taken ill just once more that term. The second time we were able to help a bit and wait out the emergency calmly, instead of thinking of ourselves.

CHERRY SAYS

Can you name some of the causes of shock?

Is a person in shock flushed or pale? Overheated or chilly? Is his pulse and breathing strong or weak?

Tell how you would take care of a person who is in a state of shock. (Read back if you're not certain. It's best to get this *right*.)

Would you ever give a drink to a person who is unconscious? Why not?

Always call a doctor at once to aid an unconscious person. Unconsciousness is a danger signal that something is wrong, except for simple fainting.

Suppose your neighbor falls down the cellar stairs and twists her ankle so painfully that she faints. How would you revive her?

What does a "live electric wire" mean? What does a "grounded object" mean?

Why should you be careful *not* to touch a victim who is in contact with a live electric wire?

Diabetics and heart patients almost always carry medicine with them. Men patients usually carry it in their right-hand jacket pockets, while women carry the necessary tablets in their handbags. If you find a person who has lost consciousness, quickly look for the medicine. By placing one tablet (or whatever the directions read) under the victim's tongue, you can check the attack.

How can you aid someone who is suffering from an epileptic attack?

Weather and Water Safety

HAVE YOU EVER SEEN A PERSON WHO HAS BEEN OUT in the hot sun, working too hard and too long? My fellow nurse and Spencer Club member, Bertha Larsen, tells this story on herself:

When she was about twelve, one hot summer day on the Larsen farm, Bertha had an argument with her older sister, May, about whether she was doing her full share of the farm chores. It was a friendly argument; her sister was half teasing. But Bertha is stubborn. She set out to "show" May who could perform the most staggering number of farm chores.

By noon, Bertha admits, she felt a little odd but would not heed her parents' and May's injunction to come indoors and rest. She stayed at work in the hot sun, figuring, "I'm a strong, skillful girl even though I'm younger than May." Suddenly, at two o'clock, it dawned on Bertha that she felt *very* odd.

Although the sun was blazing, she turned cold and clammy. Ordinarily Bertha is rosy-faced; now a farmhand advised her that she looked as "pale as a pickle." Her head ached and she felt nauseated. Weak and dizzy, she staggered to the cool shade of the barn, where her legs buckled beneath her. P.S. Sister May was not impressed. She was appalled.

What Bertha had is heat exhaustion. People can also acquire it indoors—say, in a laundry or engine room.

SALT IN HOT WEATHER

If Bertha had drunk a dozen glasses of saltwater, or had taken salt tablets in water (*and* worked in moderation), she could have avoided heat exhaustion. When a person works in a high temperature, he sweats and that helps keep his body temperature down to normal. But when you sweat a great deal, you lose the salts which are stored in your body. Without these salts, exhaustion and muscle cramps set in.

HOW TO TAKE CARE OF YOURSELF IN HOT WEATHER

Take more salt than usual, in your food and dissolved in water. Eat light, easily digested foods and eat in moderate amounts. Don't drown yourself in iced drinks! Wear loose, thin clothing. Avoid overexerting yourself during the hottest hours of the day. Perhaps you can plan to do your chores in the cool of early morning or evening.

FIRST AID FOR HEAT EXHAUSTION

If the patient is pale and clammy, breathes shallowly, feels weak and cold, have him lie down flat in a shaded place where there is cooler air circulating. Cover him lightly. Give him saltwater to drink (½ teaspoonful of salt with ⅓ glass of water), as much as he will drink. Warm coffee or tea may stimulate him. If his exhaustion doesn't pass off very soon, call a doctor.

A half teaspoon of salt in water will help restore a person suffering from heat exhaustion.

FIRST AID FOR SUNSTROKE AND HEAT STROKE

These are similar to heat exhaustion. Exposure to excessive heat outdoors causes sunstroke and to excessive heat indoors causes heat stroke. Dizziness and nausea are common to all three. However sunstroke and heat-stroke symptoms are a *flushed* face, skin *hot* and dry, no sweating, throbbing headache, a fast pulse, and high, feverish temperature.

This condition is often very serious. Send for a doctor.

First, find the patient a cool, shaded place where he can lie down and rest. Be quick, to prevent his losing consciousness. Remove as much of the patient's clothing as you conveniently can. Help him to lie down on his back, with his head and shoulders raised a little.

Now, without delay, apply cold, wet cloths or an ice bag to his head. To cool his body, wrap him in a sheet and pour on cool water, only a little at a time. Do this for two or three minutes, then stop and observe how your patient is reacting and let him rest a few seconds. Keep it up again until his skin remains cool.

Or cool his body in any convenient, quick way you can devise. Remember, his head (and that means brain) particularly must be cooled.

Important: Rub his arms and legs *toward the heart*, to stimulate circulation. Rub through the wet sheet. Rub with cold, wet cloths.

Give no stimulants. If your patient is conscious, give him drinks of cool water.

We repeat: Call a doctor at once.

Wouldn't you agree that in this instance an ounce of prevention is certainly worth a pound of cure?

FROSTBITE AND EXPOSURE TO COLD

Now let's go from hot to cold. As you know, Jack Frost can cause his own kind of damage. When the cold winds blow, watch out that he doesn't freeze your fingers and ears, or chill you so severely that you'd need medical attention.

COLD WEATHER CARE

You can avoid frostbite and numbness by dressing warmly—*woolen* socks, muffler, and mittens—no tight shoes or tight kid gloves which hamper circulation. Don't stay out too long in the cold and high wind, particularly if you feel tired or below par. Be extra careful when cold winds blow because they chill you so rapidly. Winter weather is exhilarating, but you must be prepared for it. Eat plenty of heat-producing foods like hearty soups, meat, oatmeal, butter, and sugar. Exercise helps, too.

When you go out to skate or ski, never go alone. Even an experienced athlete can have a mishap. Go with at least one companion. When you take a long, wintry walk or are planning to work outdoors in extreme cold, always let someone know where you'll be, and for about how long. If it does nothing else, it saves someone from worrying!

HOW TO RECOGNIZE FROSTBITE

Frostbite is an injury caused when a part of the body freezes. Ears, toes, fingers, nose, even cheeks are the most susceptible. If you see someone's ears turn white, or a white spot on his face, tell him so right away—for a dead white area is the sign of frostbite.

It's hard to tell about one's own ears and face. If you feel an intense coldness and numbness, take care, for that is another sign of frostbite.

WHAT TO DO

If it's your feet or hands which feel intensely cold, exercise them. If another part, such as your cheek, becomes too cold, cover it with more warm clothing or place it next to a warm surface. Keep moving around in order to keep your circulation lively.

FIRST AID FOR FROSTBITE

Arctic explorers learned, in a world of snow and ice, *not* to rub a frostbitten part with snow. This is a dangerous way to treat frozen tissues. Gangrene (poisoning) may result.

If you find someone whose feet, say, are frozen, remove his shoes and stockings, and cover his feet snugly with woolen clothing or cloth. Cover the person himself warmly. Bring him as soon as you can into a warm room, and give him a warm drink of coffee, tea, milk, or soup. Loosen any tight clothing.

Be very gentle when you handle his frozen feet, in order not to injure them still more. Dip them for a moment at a time in *lukewarm* water, not hot water. Or wrap his feet in blankets. He must thaw out gradually.

Don't use hot-water bottles or other heating devices. *Don't* place the frostbitten part near a hot stove or fireplace or radiator. *Don't* rub.

When the frostbitten feet are warm again, you should encourage your patient to exercise them. If blisters have formed, leave them alone.

FIRST AID FOR EXPOSURE TO COLD

If a person is exposed too long to extreme cold—and especially to strong winds—he may become numb, drowsy, or walk with a staggering gait. His eyesight may blur. He may fall and become unconscious.

In case he has stopped breathing, of course your first step would be to start giving artificial respiration (page 110).

You can help a person who is badly chilled by bringing him or her indoors, helping him into a bed with warm covers, and giving a warm drink. Since he is temporarily in a weakened condition, keep him away from anyone who has a cold or other infection.

DROWNING AND OTHER CAUSES OF UNCONSCIOUSNESS

In many emergencies and accidents, as we've seen, the victom may lose consciousness. He may also stop breathing. That's when artificial respiration, given by a skillful first-aider, comes to the rescue.

Here are some of the commonest cases—I'm sure you could draw up the list yourself—when a person may need artificial respiration to start him breathing again:

Drowning

Electric shock from a live wire

Breathing in gas, from a car or stove
Suffocation
Choking
Overdose of sleeping pills, or other drug

FIRST AID FOR DROWNED PERSONS

When you or the rescuers bring the drowned person out of the water, you'll do it just as quickly as possible. Carry him no farther than necessary. Quickly lay him down on his face; turn his face to one side. Start *without delay* to give him artificial respiration. (See page 110.)

If you find him lying on his back, roll him over quickly and gently. Here is a good way to turn him

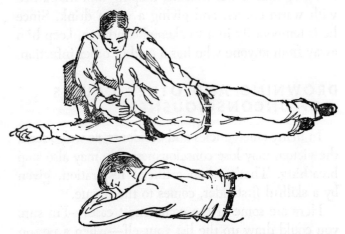

To roll patient over on his stomach, extend his right hand above his head. Then take his other hand and pull it up and towards you. As patient rolls over, place his hands under cheek.

over: Suppose he is on your left. With your left hand, take his right hand, nearest to you. Extend it above his head and hold it. Then take his other hand and gently pull toward you. As he rolls over, quickly and gently place his hands under his cheek.

After giving some artificial respiration, if he does not respond, you'd better make a *quick* inspection of his mouth, and remove seaweed, pebbles, or other material which clogs his breathing.

Pull his lower jaw forward, gently. This will bring his tongue forward and prevent it from plugging air passages. Loosen his collar and necktie.

Don't waste precious time in trying to get the water out of his lungs by rolling the victim. Artificial respiration will force the water out of his lungs.

Important: Keep the victim warm. Even on a hot day, wet clothing can chill him at a dangerous speed.

Don't delay in giving artificial respiration if he has stopped breathing or if he breathes jerkily and irregularly. Every second counts! A difference of a few seconds can lose or save a life.

Send someone for a doctor or ambulance. If you are alone with the victim, don't spend precious time calling a doctor—begin artificial respiration at once. You can save a life which, a few minutes later, even the doctor could not save.

(In Chapter XIII we'll talk about the ways you can avoid any danger of drowning when you're out swimming or boating. We'll also consider safe ways to rescue someone who is in trouble in the water—or who may be in the midst of another emergency.)

ABOUT ARTIFICIAL RESPIRATION

Way back in the Middle Ages, when a person stopped breathing, his would-be rescuers would suspend him by his heels, and blow or breathe into his nostrils. In the eighteenth century, someone invented a small bellows to force air into the nostrils and thus into the lungs. Then, in 1856, a doctor had the idea of pressing on the victim's chest, to force air in and out of the lungs that way. In 1903 another doctor improved the method, by regularly applying pressure on the victim's back. This is the basis of the method we use today. It has been improved again recently.

Here is the new method which the American Red Cross teaches. It is the Nielsen Method of artificial respiration. You *push* to send air out of the lungs (exhale), and *pull* to bring air into the lungs (inhale).

HOW TO GIVE ARTIFICIAL RESPIRATION

If you'll look at the pictures, they will help you a great deal.

1. *Position of the patient.* Place the victim lying prone (on his face). Bend his elbows and place his hands one on top of the other. Turn his head to one side, resting his cheek on his hands.

2. *Position of the first-aider.* Kneel on either your right or left knee, or both knees, in front of the patient's head. Place your hands flat on his back— thumbs almost together and fingers spread out—just below his shoulder blades.

3. *Push for exhale.* Rock forward, keeping your elbows straight. Then press down slowly and evenly on his back. This pushing forces air (and water) out of his lungs.

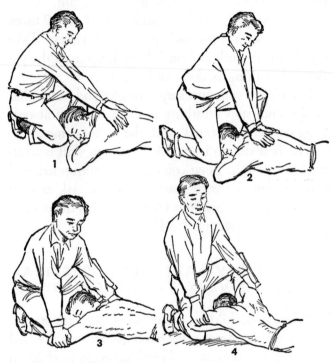

1. With elbows straight, rock forward to expel air.
2. Ease back gradually, releasing pressure.
3. Take hold of patient's upper arms.
4. Draw patient's arms up until shoulders resist.

4. *Getting ready to inhale.* Rock back, slowly and gradually easing up on your pressure. At the same time take hold of the patient's arms just above his elbows.

5. *Pull for inhale.* Draw his arms upward and toward you, until you feel his shoulders resist. Keep your own elbows straight as you rock backwards. Raising his arms pulls air into the lungs. Then lower the patient's arms to the ground, and start again.

Repeat steps 3, 4 and 5 steadily from 10 to 12 times a minute, with a second's pause in between. Take equal time to push and pull. Keep it up until the patient's breathing is deep and regular.

Even then, you must stay with him and watch that he does not stop breathing again. Keep him at rest, lying down and covered, until the doctor comes.

The best way to learn this important skill is to attend a class in it. Then you can see it performed, and you can practice with your classmates. Ask at your school, your Girl Scout or Campfire Girls troop, or at your local chapter of the Red Cross.

HOW TO GIVE ARTIFICIAL RESPIRATION TO VERY YOUNG CHILDREN

Babies and children under school age are fragile, so that you must not press too hard. Here is the Red Cross method for starting breathing again in children under four years of age.

1. Place the child lying face down, with his face turned slightly to one side, and—note this difference —with his arms at his sides.

2. Kneel on one or both of your knees, or sit, at the child's head. You may find it more convenient to place the child on a table while you work standing up.

3. Place your hands next to the child's arms. With

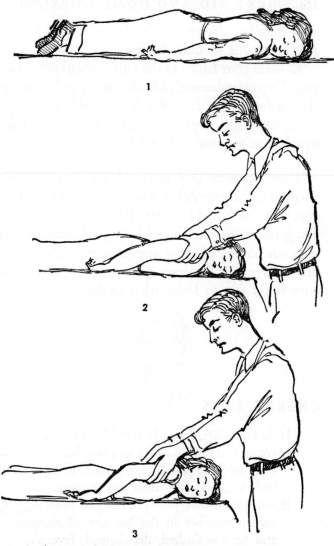

1. Arrange child on stomach, with arms at sides.
2. With hands on child's upper arms, press thumbs just below shoulder blades.
3. With hands at shoulders, raise child's chest a few inches from table.

your thumbs only, press on his back—not too hard—
just below his shoulder blades.

4. Slide your hands to the child's shoulders, place
your fingers underneath his shoulders, and raise his
chest a few inches from the floor or table top.

Repeat these steps 15 times per minute. Take
equal time to press and to lift.

There's a great deal to absorb and learn in this
chapter, isn't there? All of it is important. I hope that
you, your family and friends will have the good health
and good sense—and should I say good fortune?—to
miss out on any of these emergencies. However, in
case emergencies do occur, the very best health insur-
ance is for you to know what to do.

CHERRY SAYS

In hot weather, it's only sensible not to overexert
yourself in the hot sun or in a very hot room. Add
a salt tablet to your drinking water to replace the
body salts you lose when you perspire.

If you found that your brother had been digging
garden trenches in the hot sun all morning—
and he was flushed, dry-skinned, feverish, and
felt sick to his stomach—what condition would
you recognize? Would you be surprised if he
started to lose consciousness?

First aid for sunstroke must be given as quickly as

possible. Have the victim lie down on his back in a cool, shaded place. Apply cold, wet cloths or an ice bag to his head. Then cool his body. Call a doctor.

A dead white spot on a person's skin is a sign of frostbite. Does it help any to rub the spot with snow? How would you give gentle, gradual first aid for frostbite?

Find out where in your community you and your friends can take a course in artificial respiration.

Exactly what does artificial respiration do? Have you ever seen anyone give it?

Suppose you were about to give artificial respiration to a baby who had stopped breathing because his blankets had slipped over his head and cut off his air supply. Why would you be especially gentle and not apply too much pressure? Why would you lift up the baby's chest on each "inhale" stroke?

Do you agree with this saying? "Good health and good sense are two of life's greatest blessings."

CHAPTER X

~~~~~~

Stomach Aches and Poisons

WHEN PEOPLE SAY "STOMACH ACHE," THEY MAY mean "an old-fashioned bellyache" which is abdominal pain. Or they may really mean pain or discomfort in the stomach, usually after eating too much or an unwise mixture or eating at an unaccustomed hour.

If the pain and discomfort are located up high, and you know you have eaten too much, then you probably have indigestion. One-half or one milk of magnesia tablet taken with half a glass of water, *or* half a teaspoonful of bicarbonate of soda in half a glass of water, will help to settle your stomach. Give your stomach a rest by eating lightly and simply at the next mealtime, or by eating nothing. Drink plenty of water. Important!—take no laxatives. (I should explain to you that milk of magnesia, when taken in these very small doses, is not a laxative.)

116

ABDOMINAL PAIN

Be careful—abdominal pain can be a symptom of appendicitis. *Take no laxatives!* A laxative could rupture the appendix. Take no food or water. If the pain persists, call a doctor without delay. Rest in bed until he arrives.

Don't ignore the warning of abdominal pain. It can signal several serious conditions. If, after two or three hours, your patient continues to have abdominal pain, tenderness, nausea, vomiting, or persistent diarrhea, *get a doctor at once.* Let's repeat, *no laxatives, no food, no water.* You may apply an ice bag to relieve pain.

POISONING

Every once in a while you read in the newspaper that someone has taken a bottle off the shelf thinking it was a gargle—and mistakenly swallowed cleaning fluid, which is poison.

Usually the bottle has no label. Or some not-so-bright person has transferred cleaning fluid into an empty bottle, and not bothered to label it. Or, sometimes the original label reading "mouth wash" or "ginger ale" is left on. Unbelievable? You'd be surprised how often it happens.

Did you know that most of the victims of poisoning are small children? They are too young to read labels and to realize how dangerous it is to "taste" the contents of a strange, fascinating bottle. Elderly people, too, whose eyesight is not good, may make a mistake.

SAFETY FIRST!

Here is how you can prevent poisoning accidents:

Keep poison drugs locked up, or at least on a high shelf of the medicine cabinet—out of reach of small children.

Keep all medicines and household cleaners and other chemicals out of reach of small children.

Label all bottles correctly.

Never take medicine from an unlabeled box or bottle.

Never take medicine in the dark. Turn on the light and read the label.

Read the label three times: 1) when you take the bottle from the shelf or medicine cabinet; 2) before you pour and take it; 3) when you put the bottle back in the cabinet.

WHICH ARE POISONS?

Some drugs, like iodine or liniment, are not poisonous at all if they are applied externally, that is to the outside of the body. But they are poisonous if you swallow them.

Some medications, like aspirin or laxatives or sleeping tablets or medicines, are not poisonous if taken in the correct, prescribed amount. But if you take too much of them, they are poisonous.

Then there are poisonous chemicals, such as powerful cleaning fluids or household cleaners, insect and rat exterminators, sprays for gardens or trees, kerosene, arsenic (it's also called Paris green).

If you've had a chemistry course at school, you know that all acids (sulphuric, nitric, etc.) and all alkalies (lye or caustic soda, ammonia, etc.) are very poisonous indeed.

Now that you know which drugs and chemicals are poisonous, you are forewarned. Always handle them with caution.

SYMPTOMS OF POISONING

How can you tell if a person has swallowed poison? Let's suppose there is no empty bottle in sight to tell you, and the victim is too ill—or too young a child— to explain. Here are the symptoms you'll recognize:

Your patient will probably have stomach ache, be nauseated and throw up. He may have violent cramps and be in great pain. Yet these symptoms may not show immediately.

If he has taken certain kinds of poison, his mouth and tongue may be burned or stained.

If you see these symptoms or an emptied poison bottle, act fast.

EMERGENCY!—POISONING

Because poison can spread so quickly throughout the entire system, the first-aider must be quick, too. This is a real emergency. Call a doctor or a hospital ambulance. But give first aid at once.

FIRST AID FOR POISONING
(Except for acids and alkalies)

You have two ways to halt the poison's action:

First, dilute the poison. Give your patient water to

drink at once—five or six or seven glassfuls. Luke-warm soapy water is good, but give plain water at once while you prepare soapy water. Or, if you have baking soda right at hand, put two teaspoonfuls in each glass of water. Milk is even better, if it's there.

1 glass water + 2 tsp. baking soda = poison antidote

Second, wash out the poison by throwing it up. Having your patient drink a great deal of liquid usually will help him to vomit. If this doesn't work, give him still more water or milk to drink. Or put a finger down his throat to help bring up the poison.

After he throws up, give your patient a little warm water with—if you have it—a tablespoonful of Epsom salts in it. Have him lie down, or put him to bed until the doctor arrives.

FIRST AID FOR ACID AND ALKALI POISONS

Don't force vomiting in these cases.

If your patient has swallowed acid, give him baking soda in water, then milk. Give only moderate amounts, *not* enough to throw up. Keep him warm and watch for shock.

If your patient has swallowed alkali or lye, give him vinegar or lemon juice in water, then milk. Give only moderate amounts, *not* enough to throw up. Keep him warm and watch for shock.

A HOSPITAL EXPERIENCE

One morning when I was assigned to Emergency Ward at Spencer Hospital, our ambulance orderly brought in a man whose neighbors had found him crumpled at the bottom of a flight of stairs. At first examination Dr. "Ding" Jackson and I—I was his assisting nurse—saw the bruises and bleeding resulting from his fall. But that didn't fully explain why the man doubled up in pain. He was too exhausted to answer our questions. He seemed nauseated, not what you'd expect of a fracture. Dr. "Ding" looked at the man's mouth—it was red and sore from being burned. I examined his jacket, where some strong chemical had spilled and eaten away the fabric.

So this was a poisoning case, not primarily a fall. We gave the same first aid I've described to you above, except that Dr. "Ding" had the extra help of a stomach pump. Then male orderlies put the patient to bed in the Emergency Ward, and we let him rest.

Late in the afternoon the man woke up, weak but recovered, and told us what had happened. That morning he had gone to the refrigerator for a glass of milk. When he poured the milk out of the bottle, he thought the fluid looked watery but he was in a hurry to go to work, and drank it anyway. Then, as pain started, he remembered that his cleaning woman had a habit of transferring household disinfectant from the large, heavy jar into smaller, more convenient containers—such as a milk bottle. Without label. How this particular bottle of "milk" got into the refrigerator he did not know.

But his parting words, as he thanked us, were something about "an ounce of prevention."

FOOD POISONING

I once had a patient who was brought to the hospital critically ill from eating slightly spoiled seafood. My friend, Gwen Jones, nursed a patient who had eaten poisonous mushrooms, but the man died. And I'm sure you've heard of whole communities being laid low by food poisoning when their milk supply, the cold cuts at a picnic, or the custard pie in a lunchroom was contaminated or spoiled.

Food poisoning—mistakenly called ptomaine poisoning—occurs all year around, but mostly in the summer heat. When food is not properly refrigerated, bacteria (germs) develop in it. Bacteria develop, too, in food which is kept too long, or is exposed too long to air, and grows stale, or is exposed to flies, which carry germs.

HOW TO AVOID FOOD POISONING

You, as a future homemaker and as a person who wants to take care of her health and her family's health right now, can observe these points:

When you prepare and serve food, be sure the food, your utensils, and your hands are clean. Don't handle food if your hand or arm is infected, or if you have a very bad cold.

Keep food well refrigerated at all times. When you bring home meat and milk from the grocery store, put it under refrigeration at once. After meals, put foods in the refrigerator promptly. Be especially careful to keep cooked foods hot until they are served and to refrigerate any cooked foods which are left over. Check your refrigerator to see that it is really cold— and of course clean.

When you go on a picnic and take food with you, don't put it in the sun, and don't wait too long before serving it. Keep food covered.

Stick to pasteurized milk. If there is none where you are, boil the milk to kill any bacteria.

If you're out on a hike, look for safe water. If you can't find any, stick to bottled soft drinks.

When you eat in a restaurant, choose a clean, well-known place. Order dishes which must be freshly cooked to order. Avoid dishes masked with sauces or mayonnaise; such things as creamed seafood or meat croquettes or egg salads may be stale, even spoiled. Be careful, too, where you order hamburger and custard or cream pastries.

Pork should always be cooked well-done. Under-done pork carries trichinosis and can make you exceedingly ill. Poultry should be well-done, too.

Canned food may be left in the tin, *if* you cover and keep it under refrigeration.

Do not taste home-canned foods until they have been thoroughly heated—*boiled* is best—for at least ten minutes.

If any canned food—especially home-canned—has a disagreeable odor, or if its container or lid is bulging, destroy the food at once. Don't even taste it.

Don't eat wild mushrooms. They may be poisonous. Buy your mushrooms at the market, as they are grown expressly for market and are safe.

As for wild berries and roots, the best thing to do is to let them alone.

SYMPTOMS OF FOOD POISONING

Being sick from eating spoiled food is a thoroughly wretched business. The victim is completely exhausted, dizzy, has a headache and blurred vision, is sick to his stomach, and usually vomits. He may be ill for a few hours or as long as a week.

FIRST AID FOR FOOD POISONING

It's important to get a doctor at once. What looks like food poisoning actually may be appendicitis. And too, anyone who has food poisoning hasn't simply an upset stomach.

Put your patient to bed. Give him *no* laxatives or purgatives. Give him nothing to drink as long as he feels nauseated or throws up. Later, if he is exhausted, you may give him a little hot tea or hot clear bouillon as a stimulant. The doctor will tell you what steps to take next.

WHY MIDGE COULDN'T ATTEND
HER OWN PARTY

Midge Fortune is a doctor's daughter, and really should know better. But Midge is always in a hurry, and since she has no mother, or even any sisters or brothers to help her out, it's a wonder her scrapes aren't even worse ones.

This one started with a good idea—inviting most of her high school class over to the Fortunes' cottage for a Hallowe'en evening party. Midge didn't allow herself much time to make preparations. Even with several of her friends to help, she barely had the game equipment and the refreshments ready by the Saturday afternoon of the party.

As Midge herself admitted, she gulped down for lunch. "Just any old thing I found in the refrigerator. Some canned figs we had left and I poured cream on them. Well, I *did* notice the figs tasted a little tart. Anyway, I was in a rush."

By suppertime Midge found she could scarcely swallow, much less eat supper. She grew so dizzy and weak that she barely reached the telephone to call our house. (Her father, Dr. Fortune, was busy at Hilton Hospital.) I ran all the way to their home, and found Midge trying to imitate the whale getting rid of Jonah. She was one sick girl. I summoned the nearest neighborhood physician, Dr. Birch, and put Midge to bed.

Dr. Birch went to work on poor Midge with a stomach pump. She groaned, "First I was afraid I was going to die, and now I feel so bad I'm afraid I won't."

The saddest part, Midge said, was having to lie in

bed and hear her Hallowe'en party going on in the next room, without the hostess. All because of some slightly spoiled food.

CHERRY SAYS

The best first aid for a stomach ache is bed rest, nothing at all to eat or drink, and—if really painful—a doctor's care. *No* laxatives, *no* medicines. (If your patient has appendicitis, a laxative could rupture his appendix.)

Do you have an ice bag at your house? It can be very useful for, among other things, relieving pain in the abdomen.

Suppose you found that your little brother had helped himself to an iodine "soda." What immediate first aid would you give to the poisoned child? Of course, you'd call—or have someone else call—a doctor at once.

If you are giving first aid to someone who has swallowed poison, remember: 1) *dilute* the poison in his stomach by having him drink four to seven glasses of water, milk, or soapy water—whichever is the most handy; 2) *wash out,* that is, empty his stomach of the poison by inducing him to throw up.

If you went to a lunchroom, which would be the safer choice to order—a ham salad sandwich or a fried egg sandwich? Why?

Name at least three measures you can take in your own home to prevent food from spoiling.

CHAPTER XI

More First-Aid Know-How

TOOTHACHE

ONE ACHE I'M SURE I NEEDN'T DESCRIBE FOR YOU IS a toothache. It happens when food finds its way into the cavity of a decayed tooth. (I think candy in a cavity hurts most, don't you? And no wonder! Candy causes cavities.) Another source of toothache, usually with older people—though it can happen to anyone—is infection or a gum condition.

The rules for avoiding toothache are simple and familiar to you: Brush your teeth faithfully morning and night and, if you can, after meals. You'll brush away the leftover food particles which cause decay. Drink plenty of milk, too, for stronger, healthier teeth.

Most important, visit your dentist regularly twice a year. Don't delay and give a tiny cavity a chance to grow into a big one.

FIRST AID FOR TOOTHACHES

If you have a toothache during the day, call your dentist for an appointment at once. Pain is always a signal that something is out of order and needs repair. Even if it's a Sunday, telephone your dentist and request emergency treatment.

In case a toothache starts during the night, or a dentist is not available, you can do two things for temporary relief:

First, clean out the cavity (if there is one) with a small bit of clean cotton wrapped firmly around the end of a toothpick. Now dip a fresh piece of cotton in oil of cloves and, using a toothpick, pack it into the cavity.

Second, apply either heat or cold to the outside of your jaw. This is good when there is a cavity and especially when there is an infection, but no cavity. You'll have to try both heat and cold, and see which one helps the most.

Another emergency help is the commercially prepared dental poultices which your drugstore sells. These are medicated pads which you place against the aching tooth. Once, when I was department store nurse at Christmas time, a very cross Santa Claus from the toy department came into my infirmary with a toothache. I gave him a dental poultice and so—I hope—bolstered the hopes of the small fry who left their messages with him.

One more word: Of course these first-aid measures give only temporary relief and don't cure the toothache. See your dentist just as soon as you can.

YOUR EYES—TAKE CARE OF THEM

Your eyes are very precious, and they are irreplacable. Don't rub them, don't touch them with hands or handkerchief which are not immaculate. Use proper lighting when you read or do your homework or sew or give yourself a manicure.

Do you need glasses? It never hurts to check and find out. Sometimes a person needs glasses only for partime use, or close work. I hope you won't be too vain to wear them if you need them. A pair of red-framed glasses and a red ribbon in your hair can be pert and attractive—much more attractive than frown lines and a squint.

1 glass boiled water, cooled + ½ tsp. boric acid powder

When your eyes feel tired or scratchy—from glare, dust, or overuse—it's soothing to bathe them. Make a weak sterile solution of one-half teaspoon of boric acid powder in a glass of boiled warm water. Or use a commercial eye wash. Drop a little solution at a time into the eye from a sterilized eyedropper, not letting the eyedropper touch the eye.

Most eye doctors will advise you never to use eye cups to bathe the eyes. Their pressure is harmful, and they can carry infection.

A hot, wet compress applied to closed eyes soothes them. Use either hot water or a hot, weak boric acid solution for your compress. Sleep is the best way of all to rest your eyes.

If your eye is red, either you have a particle in the eye, or an infection such as pink-eye. Don't try to treat a reddened eye yourself. Get a doctor's help.

HOW TO REMOVE PARTICLES IN THE EYE

Warning!—if the simple method below doesn't work, see a doctor *at once*. Don't tamper with the eye, and don't let anyone but a doctor remove an embedded particle. Especially if the particle is in the eyeball, see a doctor immediately.

To remove particle from eye, grasp upper-lid eyelashes. Pull lid out and down over lower lid.

However, if you or your patient has just a speck floating in the eye, here is what to try:

1. Never examine the eyes until you have washed your hands with soap and water. Handle gently.

2. Don't rub your eyes. This will only drive the particle deeper into the eyes.

3. *Never* try to remove a particle with a toothpick, match, or any other instrument.

4. Try to wash out the particle, using a sterilized eyedropper.

Now here is a method which often works:

5. Gently pull down the *lower eyelid*. See if the

particle is lying there. If it is, you can lift it off by carefully touching the speck with the corner of a clean handkerchief or cloth. (Don't use paper cleansing tissues; their lint irritates the eye.)

6. Sometimes the particle lies inside the *upper eyelid*. Gently grasp the eyelashes of the upper lid between your thumb and forefinger. Have your patient look upward. Now, gently, pull the upper lid forward and down over the lower lid. Often this action will dislodge the speck, and tears will wash it away.

If these measures don't work, see a doctor at once.

STIES

Have you ever had a sty blossom forth on the edge of your eyelid? If you've noticed, it happens when you're not in tiptop health. Or, once in a while eyestrain causes inflammation, and that in turn produces a sty.

A sty can be quite sore. You can ease the discomfort by applying hot, wet compresses—as hot as your patient can stand it. Don't open the sty. Continue the hot wet applications, and the pus will drain off or dry out of its own accord.

CHEMICALS IN THE EYE

In case any chemicals splash into the eye, wash the eye at once and continuously with clean water. Then see a doctor.

This accident may seem unimportant at the time, but *every* accident to an eye can be serious. You have only two eyes—take care of them!

BLACK EYE

Treat a bruised eye right away. If you wait, it will discolor and then you can only wait for it to heal—of its own accord.

If the skin isn't broken, apply something cold and soft at once—an ice bag, or a piece of ice wrapped in a clean cloth, or a cold compress. Keep the eye closed during the treatment.

EARACHE

An earache can be caused by exposure to cold, or by a sudden change of altitude or a deep dive.

You may also catch cold in the ear—that is, you get an infection inside the ear. Sometimes this comes about when you have a cold in the nose or a sore throat; the infection moves into the ear as well.

When you have a cold in the ear, don't blow your nose too hard. Don't close off one nostril and close your mouth while blowing. You'll spread the infection this way.

FIRST AID FOR EARACHE

If the earache is due to a cold, go to bed and take care of the cold. Apply heat to the ear—a hot water bottle or an electric heating pad. If you find that heat doesn't relieve the earache, try cold (but dry) applications.

If the earache is due to exposure to cold, or a dive, apply heat or cold.

When the earache is severe or persists, it may be an infection. This can lead to diseases of the ear and the mastoids and some degree of deafness. See your doctor promptly.

If there is a foreign body in the ear, only a doctor should remove it.

HICCUPS

Hiccups are supposed to be funny or ridiculous, as if sounding off every few seconds were a joke. But hiccups can give you an uncomfortable wrench and if they persist, may require a doctor's care. One of my patients hiccupped for two days before she realized she'd better see a doctor, and *she* did not think it was in the least funny. She was exhausted.

For most of us, first aid for hiccups consists of slowly sipping a glass of cold water, a sip at a time. Sometimes it helps if you hold both eardrums closed as you swallow. Or add half a teaspoonful of baking soda to the water.

Another way to stop hiccups is to hold your breath.

Still another way is to fit a paper bag tightly over your face, and breathe in and out. The carbon dioxide which accumulates often will check the hiccups.

One of the best ways is simply to lie down and rest.

CRAMPING IN FEET AND LEGS

Have you ever been in swimming, and been seized by a sudden, painful cramp in your feet or legs? (My brother, Charlie, says you can avoid this if, when you first walk into the water, you go in on tip-

toe.) Or does your foot and leg "fall asleep" occasionally—or does your hand cramp after several hours of
writing examination papers?

Lie down, if it is the feet or legs which are
cramped. Apply hot wet towels. Massage the cramped
muscles, rubbing toward the trunk. You'll stimulate
circulation in this way, and smooth out the tensed
muscles.

CHOKING

One of our family jokes is that my grandmother
seems to be at her most talkative and argumentative
whenever fish with a great many bones is being served
for dinner. Invariably we say, "Now please, let's defer
some of the conversation and pay attention to those
fishbones." Invariably my grandmother refuses and,
within a few minutes, she is red in the face and gasping for breath—having choked on a fishbone. We are
all sure that when she joins the angels, it will be with
the aid of a fishbone.

Choking is painful and may cut off the air supply
if you can't stop it. Swallowing an unswallowable object may cause it. Or have you ever gulped something and had it slide into your windpipe instead of
your throat?

When a foreign object becomes lodged in the
throat, windpipe, or food passage (esophagus), do
this:

Hold the viction with his head between his knees.
Now give him a sharp slap on the back. This may dislodge the offending object.

Don't try to remove the obstruction with your finger. Don't try to push it down with food, such as mashed potato. Removing it is a job for the doctor.

A sharp slap on the back will often dislodge food caught in the throat.

Occasionally, even after the victim coughs up the foreign body, you may need to give artificial respiration.

If the victim can't cough up the obstruction and has serious difficulty in breathing, call a doctor. This is an emergency.

You can safeguard small children by keeping out of their reach such things as safety pins, loose buttons, coins, large pieces of hard candy. Very small children have a special talent for swallowing these things.

INHALING GAS

You probably know that carbon monoxide gas, coming from automobile exhausts or leaks from gas stoves, is a troublemaker if you inhale it. The difficulty is, carbon monoxide is colorless and nearly odorless, so that it is hard to detect escaping gas.

The first hint a person may have that he has inhaled gas is when he finds himself yawning and with a headache. If he continues to inhale carbon monoxide, dizziness, nausea, weariness and ringing in the ears will probably follow, and then fluttering of the heart. He may notice these symptoms gradually, or they may come on so suddenly that he finds he cannot walk or crawl.

WHAT TO DO

Get the patient into fresh air as quickly as you can. If it is summer, you may decide to help him outdoors or, if the weather is cold, into a room with warm clean air. A patient may collapse if he is taken abruptly from a warm, gas-filled room into cold, wintry air. So use your own good judgment.

If your patient is gasping, or has stopped breathing, give him artificial respiration at once.

Call a doctor. Sometimes victims of gas need oxygen, which a doctor gives with an inhalator.

CHERRY SAYS

The next time you visit your dentist, ask him how best to care for your teeth and gums.

What can you do to remove a particle from your eye? What should you *not* do?

If the particle doesn't come out of your eye easily and soon, call your doctor without delay.

In case of an earache, will heat or cold give the most relief?

Why is it important not to blow your nose too hard when you have an earache?

Name three ways you can stop hiccups. Can you name four?

If a person is choking on something he has swallowed, what can you do to help him?

Describe the two characteristics of carbon monoxide that make it so difficult to detect.

How would you revive a person who had inhaled gas, but is still breathing? How would you help him if he were not breathing?

~~~~~~

CHAPTER XII

Safety First At Home

BE SAFETY-WISE!

"I'M NOT GOING TO HAVE ANY ACCIDENTS," EVERY one of us thinks, and sometimes says. "*I'm* not going to get caught in a fire. *My* mother isn't likely to fall off our stepladder. *My* baby brother isn't going to drink cleaning fluid by mistake. Those things happen to other people. Not ever to anyone I know, usually."

Yes, we all think that. But none of us is immune.

Have you ever seen an accident? Especially one which could have been prevented if someone hadn't been careless or daredevil or just plain ignorant?

Or have you ever visited a friend or relative who was slowly recovering from an accident? Then you know the high costs involved.

You can safeguard your own life and health, and your family's, as well. You can help prevent suffering, and the time, labor, and expense which accidents cost. You can even save lives, if you will help prevent accidents.

DID YOU KNOW—

—that about ten million accidents happen every year in the United States?

—that about one hundred thousand people die as a result? And thousands more are handicapped or disfigured for the rest of their lives?

—that home accidents account for about one-third of all fatal accidents?

—that automobile and traffic accidents account for another third of the deaths?

—that many people lose their lives every year because of burns, scalds, and drowning?

—that boys have more accidents than girls, and more serious accidents?

—that of all age groups, children aged one to four and elderly persons are the ones most often injured?

—that more American civilians are killed during peacetime at home, at work, and on streets and highways than American soldiers in combat during wartime?

These figures come from The National Safety Council. I hope they impress you. One of the most important things you can do every single day, is to help prevent accidents from ever happening in the first place.

SAFETY AT YOUR HOUSE

Most of us think of home as a place of safety and refuge. Yet, as we've just seen, home accidents cause almost as many deaths as automobile accidents, and a great many more injuries. It's up to you, as well as the other members of your family, to make and keep your home a truly safe place—because no one else can do it for you.

The most frequent accidents at home are falls.

How many safety hazards can you find in this picture?

People trip and fall over an electric cord, fall off a shaky stepladder, stumble and slip on a child's ball, tumble down cellar stairs, especially in the dark.

Other common home accidents arise from frayed electric cords, gas leaks, poisonous materials swallowed by mistake, scissors and knives left lying around, window or rug repairs deferred too long and —well, carelessness.

Do any of these hazards exist in your house? How alert are you to everyday danger? How observant?

After you check this list from memory, try making an experiment:

Taking the list with you, walk around your house, and observe, and check again *at first-hand*. Next, look in your yard and garage or barn, or in the hallway and stairs of your apartment house, and check here. How many *more* hazards do you find?

Can you, now that you are alerted, discover a hazard which you never knew existed before? Perhaps you'll find some which are not on our check list, too.

Incidentally, can you think of any hazards in your own room?

It's a good idea to talk over all these hazards with your family. While it may cost a few extra dollars to re-wire the lamps or install an extra basement stair rail, the cost will be far less than the cost of an accident.

YOU AND YOUR FAMILY

Your home is *yours*, no one else's. Your home is what you and all your family make it. How pleasant and attractive it is depends—not on what you can spend—on how much consideration, cooperation, and imagination you and your family give and have for one another.

See if you can't persuade your family to think and do something about preventing accidents at home. It's essential that your home be a safe and healthful place to live in. You can make a real contribution by bringing to their attention hazardous places in and around your house. Then you can suggest safety measures.

BELIEVE IT OR NOT

Tom Stetson, whose house is across the street from ours, pried open a milk container using a carving knife. The knife slipped and cut an artery in Tom's wrist. Fortunately Dr. Birch was at home when it happened.

A friend's grandmother, who is seventy years old, has a storage shelf above the cellar stairs, opposite the door to the cellar stairs. You can reach the shelf only by standing on tiptoe and reaching across the open flight of stairs. The old lady hasn't fallen yet, but chances are she will.

At our school cafeteria, when I was a high school student, Betty Lou spilled a cup of soup on the floor right in front of the cashier's desk. Because we were all in a hurry, no one instantly mopped up the wet spot. Two of us on line in back of Betty Lou slipped and sat down hard, *very* hard. I did something or other to my back, had to go to the doctor, and limped for a week.

Silver Boy, the Trent's collie, ate a whole package of sweet laxative tablets which someone left lying open on a window sill. That was the last of Silver Boy.

You see, I'm sure, how unnecessary such accidents are. Be safety-wise. Many accidents *can be prevented*.

HOW TO PREVENT BURNS AND SCALDS

Burns and scalds are, for the most part, *preventable*. Did you know that they cause the death of more young children than any other kind of accident? And of people over sixty-five? The rest of us are not immune, either.

You'll do yourself and your family a real service if you remember and practice these rules:

Never pour water on flaming grease. Turn off the gas. Then extinguish the flames with salt, sand, or baking soda. Or cover the flames with a metal lid.

Never pour kerosene into a wood or coal stove, even if you think the fire is out. Never use kerosene to start a fire.

Never put pans of hot water or coffee or other liquid too near the edge of the stove—or the sink or table. And keep small children away from any container of hot liquid.

Keep matches out of reach of children. Close the cover of your matchbook before striking.

When you attach an electric cord to the toaster, percolator, or iron, place the cord where no one will trip over it and jerk it out.

Some dry cleaning fluids will burst into flame if

rubbed vigorously or held near a flame, or will explode. Read the label carefully before you buy. The words flammable, inflammable, and combustible all mean the same thing: capable of bursting easily into flame. Look for the word non-combustible on the label.

Get the picking-up habit at home. Trash lying around invites a fire.

Don't let clothing or curtains come too near, or blow into, an open fire. If it's a fireplace at home, a metal fire screen is a good protection, especially for young children. If it's a bonfire, don't go too close and keep young children at a safe distance.

If you'll be alert and responsible and do these things, you can really prevent some serious injuries from ever happening.

IN CASE OF FIRE

Sometimes, in spite of our best efforts, an accident does happen. Then we can help ourselves and others by knowing the most effective, safest methods of rescue.

The first rule in any emergency is to keep calm and use your intelligence. In case of fire, you'll need to use clear thinking and speed.

1. What would you do if, suddenly and without warning, your clothes caught fire? You'd roll yourself up in a rug or blanket to smother the flames. Smother from the shoulders toward the feet. If no rug or blanket were at hand, you'd lie down and slowly roll over and over, to smother the flames. You'd also beat out the flames with any cloths you could reach, or with your hands.

What would you *not* do, if your clothes caught fire? You wouldn't run, because running fans the flames. You wouldn't stand up, because you'd be likely to inhale the flames. You'd lie or crawl on the floor where the air is coolest.

2. Suppose you were in a burning building, although the room you were in was not yet on fire. What would you do? You'd quickly close all doors and windows in the room. Then you'd figure out the safest way to escape. Perhaps you could safely climb out through the window. Perhaps you'd decide to wait for the firemen. In order to breathe while you waited, when the room grew airless, you'd open one window a few inches, staying close to the floor. You'd cover your face with a wet cloth, if possible.

Now let's consider a still more dangerous situation.

3. Suppose, in order to save yourself or rescue a small child, you had to escape from or through a burning room. Exactly how would you do it?

You'd crawl along the floor where the air is coolest. You wouldn't stand up because you'd breathe in hot air. You'd try to protect your face and hands. Use gloves or towels or cloths for your hands, if you have them. Cover your head with a hood made of a coat or towel, to protect yourself against flame.

To protect yourself against breathing in gas fumes (carbon monoxide) and possibly flames, you'd cover your nose and mouth with your handkerchief, scarf, or other cloth. Wet, if you could safely manage it. This helps protect you from breathing in irritating gas fumes and possibly flames. *But* a handkerchief is not a gas mask. Don't think you can safely enter a smoky area simply because of the handkerchief.

4. How would you escape from the burning room into a hallway or down the stairs?

Be careful! Open doors and windows cautiously; opening them might make a draft which would fan the fire. If a door into a hallway or stairway feels hot, don't open it. Superheated air may have collected on the other side, and it is dangerous to take a breath of it.

Feel the door first. Keep down very low and brace yourself, because hot air currents may force the door wide open. It will be hard to close again if you see that a hot, smoky hallway or stairs is not a safe route of escape.

5. The best thing you can do, if there's no safer way, is to escape through a window. Make a rope by firmly tying together sheets and blankets. Then fasten one end securely to a heavy piece of furniture or a heavy steam pipe, and slide down the rope to safety. First, though, give rescuers a chance to reach you.

Don't jump from a window. Try to attract the attention of the rescuers. Firemen can do some pretty wonderful things, you know.

IN CASE OF ESCAPING GAS

When there's a fire, there's also carbon monoxide gas, floating in the heated air and smoke. Gas can poison anyone who breathes it. It can leak out of gas stoves, automobile exhausts, gas heaters, gas meters.

And it's so easy not to be aware of the colorless, almost odorless gas! Here's where your knowing rescue methods may come in handy.

One word, first, about old wells, silos, and a cave's inner passages. The "dead air" in these places may not contain enough oxygen to keep you alive. They are full of carbon monoxide gas. Don't go into them. You could lose consciousness without warning. No adventure is worth that high a price.

Here are some vital *do's* and *don'ts:*

Don't ignore any hint of escaping gas. Call up your gas company promptly and report the leak. They will send a repairman. Meanwhile, open windows wide and ventilate your house.

Don't strike matches or let anyone carry a lighted candle or cigarette into a place where you know or suspect gas is escaping. Use a flashlight when you search for a gas leak.

Do know the location of the gas meter in your house. Ask your father to show you how to turn it off in case of emergency, such as leaks or broken pipes or a flood.

Do always, when you light the stove, strike the match *before* you turn on the gas.

Don't let pots with liquid boil over on the stove. The liquid will put out the flame and gas will escape.

Don't leave a gas flame burning in a room where anyone is sleeping.

Don't sit in a parked car with the windows closed and the engine running. Gas from the exhaust will have no place to escape, and you'll breathe it in.

Don't run an automobile engine in a closed garage.

Don't breathe gas, even for the shortest time. It will weaken you, if not overcome you. A wet handkerchief tied over your nose and mouth is *not* a gas mask. It will keep out smoke, but it will *not* save your life.

RESCUING GAS VICTIMS

If you must rescue someone from a gas-filled room, first open all doors and windows in your house. Break the windows if you have to. Be quick. You yourself must stay out of the gas-filled room while it ventilates. Only then is it safe for you to enter and quickly help the victim out of there.

If the victim is overcome in a small garage, you can open the garage door, take a deep breath of clean air and hold it, while you quickly pull him out.

HOW TO AVOID ELECTRIC SHOCK

It's easy to avoid an electric shock, if you know how. If you don't know, or are careless—watch out! Here's how:

Don't touch a bare electric wire outdoors or indoors.

Don't touch a frayed electric wire. It's bare, too. Have it repaired or buy a new electric cord.

Don't touch an electric socket—because there's free-flowing electricity coming out.

You must be extra careful not to touch any of these *and* a grounded metal object at the same time. "Grounded" means anything touching the ground, directly or indirectly. Kitchen sinks, washbowls, bathtubs, radiators are "grounded" because they have metal pipes extending to the ground.

Don't touch any turned-on radio, toaster, electric lamp or switch, or other electrical appliance if your hands or body are wet or if the floor is wet. Nor if you are holding or touching a metal object. You may receive a shock. Of course don't touch the inside wires of these things, either, while they are turned on.

Don't have a tangle of extension cords in your house.

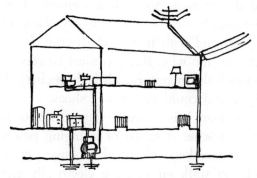

Household fixtures which have pipes that extend into the ground are dangerous conductors of electricity.

RESCUING ELECTRIC SHOCK VICTIMS

It's dangerous, unless you know exactly how, to try to rescue a victim from contact with a live wire. Be extremely careful.

First, shut off the current. Pull the electric wire out of the socket. Two cautions! Grasp the electric cord where it is not bare or wet. At the same time you must not touch grounded objects.

Another way to turn off the current is to pull the main switch in the house or building—if you can do so quickly. Otherwise phone, or ask someone to phone, the electric company to turn off the power.

If these methods aren't safe enough or quick enough, take a *dry* towel, sheet, or garment and— without touching the wire—encircle the wire with it. Now pull the wire away from contact with the victim. You could also use a dry board, or dry rope, or a dead dry stick. Stand on something dry.

And if *that* won't work, here's another way, but a riskier one. Stand on something dry. Take a towel or garment and with it drag the victim away from contact with the wire. But you must be very careful not to touch the victim, for his body is charged with electricity and could give *you* a shock.

Out of doors it is extremely dangerous for you to attempt a rescue. A fallen or swinging power line carries tremendous electrical voltage; even the ground you walk on may be electrically charged. Keep away! Call the electric company, the police or the fire department as quickly as you can.

Indoors a bathroom is a very dangerous place from which to try to rescue an electric shock victim. That's because a bathroom contains several grounded objects, and damp objects, often a wet floor. Don't attempt this rescue, or you may become a victim yourself. Turn off the main power switch first, or call the electric company to do so.

IF LIGHTNING STRIKES

Lightning can give you an electric shock but this risk, too, can be forestalled. If lightning strikes **very** near you, when you're indoors, stay away from fireplaces and chimneys and open windows, all of which create a draft. Avoid stoves and any other metal object. Lightning rods installed on your house are a good protection.

If you're outdoors when lightning flashes nearby, the safest place is inside an automobile with a steel top, or a cave, or a thick woods. Or just lie down in a hollow in the ground. An isolated tree or a small exposed wooden house *look* like shelter, but they aren't.

POISONING ACCIDENTS

One of the easiest home accidents to prevent is that of taking poisonous materials by mistake. The rules are simple common sense:

Make it a practice to read the label before taking or administering any drug or medicine. Have plenty of light on.

Label all drugs and cleansers and chemicals correctly.

Keep all poisonous materials locked up on a high shelf where small children can't reach them. Even drugs like aspirin and laxatives should be kept out of reach.

CHERRY SAYS

What would be your own definition of "safety-wise?"

A good first-aider's job is not only to help people when they are hurt, but to prevent accidents before they can happen.

Make a list of the places and things in your house which could cause someone to fall.

If your grandparents live with you, think of three steps you can take to make your house a safer and more comfortable place for them. Even though they may be vigorous people, still their eyesight may not be as sharp or their muscles as quick and limber as your own.

What would you do in case your clothes caught fire? What would you *not* do?

What action would you take if you were caught in a burning building? (After you answer this, read back and make very certain that you're right. It's important.)

Would you use a match or flashlight in searching for a gas leak?

Call your gas or electric company promptly and report any emergency or any hint of leaks or disrepair. The utilities companies will send repairmen and, if necessary, an emergency crew.

Name as many ways as you can think of to avoid receiving an electrical shock.

Don't touch any turned-on electric appliance if your hands or body are wet or if you're standing on a wet floor. Your body would serve as a circuit linking the electricity and water, and you would receive a shock.

~~~~~~~~~~~~~~~~~~~~~~~~~~~~~~~~~~~~~~

CHAPTER XIII

Outdoor Safety

YOU SPEND A LARGE PART OF YOUR TIME AT SCHOOL. It's worth your while to cooperate with your school teachers, monitor, and the traffic officer on your school street. The rules are made for your own safety, and the safety of others.

At a movie house, or other public building, it's a good idea to note where the nearest exit is. Where many people are gathered, don't hurry or push or run. In case of a public emergency, remain calm and orderly. Your example will be a help to others. Follow the instructions of the persons who are in charge of clearing the building safely.

SAFETY ON THE STREETS

You may not drive yet; you are a pedestrian. But did you know that pedestrians cause a large percentage of automobile accidents? You dart out in the middle of the block from behind a parked car—and a driver jams on his brakes in order not to hit you.

The driver in back of him isn't expecting a sudden stop, and he runs into the first car. Result: a collision.

In some cities jaywalking is punishable by a sizable fine. Don't you think that's right? If drivers have to obey traffic laws, shouldn't pedestrians (who are part of traffic) have to obey them, too?

Observe traffic laws, lights, markers. Await the policeman's or motorman's signal. Wait on the sidewalk or in safety zones, not on the curb. Look both ways before crossing. Don't cross a corner diagonally. Don't try to beat a car across the street. When you're on your bicycle, don't go too fast or too close to cars. Don't hitch onto a car.

You have only one life, and only one sound, healthy body. Please keep them.

SAFETY IN BICYCLING

So many girls and boys enjoy riding their bicycles for sport that The Bicycle Institute of America has worked out a *Safe Riding Code*. You probably observe most of the rules already, but if you'd like a copy, write to The Bicycle Institute at 122 East 42nd Street, New York City. They have some interesting tips for you. For instance, wear light-colored clothes (or something white) when you cycle at night, so that you'll be easily visible to motorists. Some others —besides obeying all traffic regulations—are:

—always signal before making turns
—walk across heavy traffic
—ride out of driveways slowly and cautiously
—ride single file, and don't weave

—never stunt or race in traffic

—check your bicycle brakes and light periodically

The Bicycle Institute also offers some unusual ideas for bicycle outings and rodeos for you and your friends.

SAFETY IN SWIMMING

Can you swim? It's such fun and makes you feel so good that I hope you are a skilled swimmer, or will learn to be. Once you become a good swimmer, you can take full part in such other water sports as canoeing, sailing, water skiing, and water ballet.

Being a swimmer is the one and only way to be safe in, or on, the water. It's astonishing to me that some young people have never learned to swim. For instance, my pilot friend, Wade Cooper, a strapping young man, admitted he could not swim. He admitted this one evening while he was thrashing and gasping in the water. He'd taken me canoeing in the moonlight. Our canoe overturned, and I had to rescue Wade and tow him to safety. When we reached shore, Wade was indignant at being rescued by a girl. It took him a week to forgive me for saving his life. He did promise me to learn to swim, though.

In case you want to learn, the Red Cross has swimming classes wherever you live. Your school or Y probably has a swimming pool and lessons. Be sure to get good instruction, so that you won't have any poor habits to unlearn.

If you already know how to float, tread water, and swim, you probably know something else—how to use your good judgment in the water. How many of these safety measures do you *always* observe?

Swim in water which is clean—preferably in water certified to be clean by your local Board of Health. Public bathing beaches and pools are a good choice.

Swim in safe water—no strong currents, no underground rocks, reefs, tree stumps, or pits.

Swim where a lifeguard is on duty at all times.

Swim only when you feel well and warm—not chilled, not overheated, either.

Wait at least two hours after a meal before you swim.

Swim with another good swimmer, never alone, even in a pool. A companion can give you instant help in case you need it. On a long swim, have a skilled swimmer in a boat accompany you.

Don't swim out too far or in water too deep or waves too powerful for your swimming skill. Don't accept dares or tempting invitations to swim into areas not safe for *you*. Remember you'll have the problem of swimming back.

If you begin to feel tired or chilled, leave the water right away. Rest and keep warm. (Stay out of the blazing sun, though.)

Before you dive, check the water depth first.

HOW TO RESCUE A DROWNING PERSON

Only a trained lifesaver can afford to risk a swimming rescue of a drowning person. Don't *you* swim out to save him.

You can be a great help, though, by using other methods which will not jeopardize your own life.

Many people start to drown only a few feet from the beach or dock, in water just a little over their heads. From a safe place, you can push or throw to him something he can hang on to, while you pull on its other end. Thus you can pull him in to safety. Here is a list of possible things to use: a pole or a strong branch, a shirt or other long garment, a towel, or towels firmly knotted together to form a rope.

A pole or strong branch can often be used to make a rescue from shore.

Or if a life preserver is handy, throw it to him. It will keep him afloat and he can paddle to safety. If you have no life preserver, shove or throw something that will float, such as a large plank or an oar. If he hangs onto this, it too will keep him afloat.

Another safe rescue method—if you know how to handle a boat—is for you to row out to him in a rowboat, a steady one with oars. Be careful that the drowning person in his fright does not pull you out of the boat into the water. Don't let him climb in from the side. Back up the boat to him. Extend him

When making a rescue from a boat, always pull the victim to the stern. Climbing aboard from the side can tip the boat.

an oar rather than your hand. Hold the boat steady as he climbs in. Or he can hold on as you row him to shore. If the water is rough or at high tide, don't attempt this type of rescue.

If you yourself are in trouble in the water, a simple, safe thing to do is roll over on your back and float. You can float indefinitely (once you've learned how), and sooner or later the water will carry you ashore at some point. Floating gives you a chance to rest, too, so that you can resume your swim.

SAFETY IN BOATING

Whether you handle a canoe, a rowboat, or a sailboat, here again it's better to be safe than sorry.

Before you go out on the water, learn how to swim and learn how to handle your boat. Never go alone. Don't go in the dark. Keep your boat in good repair.

If you are going on a long boating trip, study weather reports first for storm warnings, and carry a life preserver for every member of your group.

Don't overload your boat. In a rowboat, use oars, not planks or a pole. You and your companions should distribute your weight evenly in the boat, with one person to a seat. In a canoe, balance your weight, and sit or kneel in the bottom of the canoe. Don't stand up or move around. If you decide to change places, come to shore or shallow water to do so.

If you capsize, it's safest to cling to your overturned boat until help arrives. The swim back may be farther than you estimate, and your watersoaked clothes will hamper your swimming.

Of course always tell one or more responsible persons in advance that you are going boating, where and in what direction, and about when you expect to be back.

SAFETY IN ICE SKATING

If you own a pair of ice skates, you either think they are the best, or you have your eye on another, better pair you plan to have. Straight steel blades are the easiest to skate on, while curved runners are fine for figure skating. Just be sure that your shoes are firmly laced across your instep and ankle.

Any risk in ice skating arises in *where* you choose to skate. You know you're safe when you skate on an indoors rink or on an outdoors rink which is open only when the ice is in good condition.

How can you judge whether a pond or river is safe to skate on? Look for ice which is four to six inches thick, clear and hard, and safe to skate on. Keep off the ice if you see white spots; they are air holes. Watch out for snow, ice, and slush because these mask air holes.

It's safest to skate close to shore, since the ice farther out may be thin. After a thaw, you must make sure that the ice will support you and your friends.

HIKING AND CAMPING SAFELY

When I was a camp nurse, I was lucky enough to go along on an overnight camping trip with some of my young friends among the Intermediates, led by our Nature Counselor. It turned out to be an unexpectedly eventful twenty-four hours. Aside from that, we all thoroughly enjoyed hiking and cooking and sleeping outdoors. Have you ever gone with your friends or your Girl Scout troop on a hiking or camping trip? Do you know the basic safety rules for living outdoors?

First there's the matter of getting from civilization to where you're headed. That usually means hiking along a highway in traffic. Walk on the left side of the road, so that you can see and avoid oncoming cars. Be watchful at curves and hilltops. If you're hiking at dusk or at night, wear something white so that motorists can see you. It doesn't hurt to carry a lighted flashlight either. Keep away from railroad tracks, swamps, quicksand.

Don't drink out of a stream unless you know its water has been analyzed and declared clean to drink. It's safest to carry tap water in your canteen. If you must use water from an untested stream, boil it for ten minutes before you drink it. Boiling will kill any germs which the water may contain. (Buying bottled soda pop is a pleasant, safe solution.)

Take along your first-aid kit. Take along a flashlight, matches, whatever special equipment you plan to use. Too much can be a burden, though.

Learn the safe way to build a fire. Never start a fire with kerosene. Learn how to douse a fire until fire site and earth are cold. It's fun to learn how to cook over a campfire, and it makes you that much more self-reliant, too. Let wild mushrooms, berries, and roots alone; they may be poisonous.

When you are tired, stop and rest. It pays to rest for five or ten minutes every hour. Sit down or lie down, putting some dry material or garment under you.

SAFETY ON THE FARM

Do you live on a farm? Or have you ever visited a real, working farm? If you have, you know farms are vitally interesting, productive places. You also know that dangers exist, with all the tools, machinery, animals, specialized buildings and equipment there are around a farm.

It's doubly important for you to have safety know-how on a farm since you may be some distance from neighbors, doctor, hospital, fire department, and gas and electric companies. You can be a great help on a farm by helping to prevent accidents, and taking safety measures like these:

Keep away from machine gears and machine knives, such as corn huskers, shredders, reapers, belts and pulleys. All these things should be equipped with guard shields and covers.

Learn the safe way to use such everyday farm tools as a knife, axe or hatchet, garden shears, hammer, and others. When you use sharp cutting tools, always cut away from you.

Avoid shaky ladders, nails in boards, open cisterns, rakes or saws or other sharp tools which may be left about.

Watch out that even a friendly animal, if he is frightened or startled, does not kick, bite or gore you. Easy does it—but keep your distance. Be careful with a strange animal and animals with young.

Don't light a match in a barn. Kerosene, gasoline, and other combustible liquids should be labeled and safely stored. (Many farmers store them in red metal containers.) Learn the safe way to use your oil heater.

With your family, work out a plan of what you all would do in case of fire on the farm. Choose safe exits. You might decide to buy several fire extinguishers, and keep them in strategic places.

IT'S UP TO YOU

Do you recognize these invitations to having an accident?— "I dare you!" "Who cares if it's dangerous?" "Let's play a practical joke on him."

These are famous last words. Sometimes (I can vouch for this out of my nursing experience) they are the passport to a nice, long, painful stay in the hospital.

Dares, recklessness, wild pranks—all have a high cost and never are worth it. There are much better ways to enjoy yourself, and surer paths to popularity.

HOW'S YOUR STATE OF MIND?

Have you ever grown so flustered when you were getting dressed for a party that you dropped your bottle of toilet water on the tile bathroom floor and cut your hand picking up the pieces?

Have you ever been so worried or upset that you raced out of the house, leaving the stove lighted and unattended?

Have you ever let yourself grow so overtired that you broke everything you touched or stumbled from sheer exhaustion?

I won't even mention thoughtlessness or poor

judgment, since I'm sure you're too mature for such tricks as holding pins or tacks in your mouth, or hanging out the window of a moving car. Tricks like these are not merely foolish—they may be fatal.

Remember to keep calm.

Remember to use your good judgment.

Be safety-wise!

CHERRY SAYS

Do you always hike along the highway *facing* oncoming cars? Do you always wear something white at night when hiking or bicycling? Is your bike fitted with a light?

If you know how to swim, do you also know your limits? Do you know how to tread water?

Whether you swim, wade, or merely dunk yourself, choose clean water which is free of underwater hazards. Be sure there is a lifeguard on duty.

Always swim, boat, ice skate with at least one companion. Tell your family where you are going, and when to expect you back.

Learn to swim before you go boating or sailing.

If you are out boating and your boat overturns, what should you and your friends do?

How can you judge when a pond is frozen solidly enough to be safe to skate on?

If you live on a farm, can you name the types of accidents that are most common in a rural community? How can you help to prevent them?

CHAPTER XIV

What Is a Home Nurse?

WHEN A MEMBER OF YOUR FAMILY IS ILL, YOU'LL want to do your share toward helping him or her get well quickly. Your mother will have the main responsibility of nursing. But besides the bedside nursing, there are many other necessary chores to be done. All the members of your household will divide up these jobs in order to help Mother.

A JOB FOR EVERYONE

You and your sister and brother will have special responsibilities delegated to each of you. For instance, your sister can keep an eye on the younger children. You will help with the meals and answer the telephone. Your brother can take charge of errands and repair jobs. Your father can market for groceries. (Of course this is just an example.) Everyone can make his own bed and keep his room tidy. All these things will help free Mother to do the nursing.

NO ONE IS TOO LITTLE TO HELP

Once, when I was a private duty nurse, I stayed on a farm and nursed a farmer's wife, Jessie Tucker, who had pneumonia. The farmer, John Tucker, was busy all day in the fields, but the Tuckers' children were a great help to me. Ruth, who was eight, mothered the younger children and helped me nurse— and cook. Sam, aged six, was Home Guard in case visitors arrived, and he also brought water as we needed it. Susie, five, collected the mail and told stories to Sparky, aged one-and-a-half. Sparky's job was to talk nicely to the baby, Marietta, and help rub her back at bath time. (Marietta, three months old, was the only one without a job.) The neighbors helped, too, when they could. But it was the Tucker children who made it easier for me to nurse their mother back to good health.

WHAT *YOU* CAN DO

Special occasions may arise when you will be your mother's right-hand aid. She may need you as her "second pair of hands" when she gives the patient medicine or applies a compress. You may even give certain treatments yourself. You might be particularly skilled at setting up attractive trays for the invalid. Or you may be the one who, with games or reading, provides the best boost to the patient's morale. There are ever so many ways in which you can help to take the burden off Mother.

YOUR OWN HEALTH

A home nurse, like any other nurse, must keep healthy. It's good sense to go to your doctor for a yearly checkup, and visit your dentist every six months. Follow a good regimen: the right foods, enough sleep, outdoor exercise.

A nurse must take time to safeguard her own health. Can you imagine a good nurse with a cold? If your shoes, stockings, or clothes get wet or even damp, change at once into dry ones. Try to avoid exposure to extremes of weather. To get over a cold, get extra sleep, keep warm, drink plenty of liquids, especially orange juice. And, in general, don't take patent medicines, nor habitually dose yourself (or others) with remedies.

If you are going to nurse, or help nurse, a member of your family who has a contagious illness, the doctor will vaccinate you beforehand. Vaccination renders you immune to contagion for a time.

PERSONAL HYGIENE

A home nurse, like any other nurse, must be clean and neat. It isn't necessary to tell you, I'm sure, about a daily bath or shower, fresh clothes, and a weekly shampoo. Your hair as a home nurse has to be neat, not flying. Don't touch your hair, particularly in the sickroom and in the kitchen.

WASH YOUR HANDS

A good nurse has to have clean hands at all times. Because it's so easy to carry infectious matter on one's hands, be sure to wash them after you care for your patient or touch anything soiled.

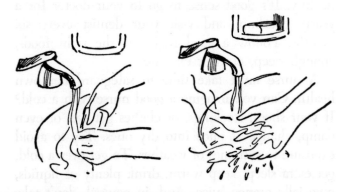

To protect both you and your patient, scrub your hands often throughout the day.

Before you give treatment or medication or touch your patient's food, check to make sure that your hands are clean. Even a doorknob or a light switch may not be clean, so watch what you touch.

Before and after you tend your patient, wash, wash, wash your hands! Here's how:

Roll up your sleeves and remove your wristwatch and jewelry. Wash your hands under running water, or pour water from a container. Hot water is best. Use plenty of soap, scrub and rinse well. Wash your hands twice over—under your fingernails, too. Dry your hands on a clean towel. Paper towels are handy.

WHAT A HOME NURSE WEARS

A bright, cheerful, washable dress with short sleeves is best to wear when nursing a patient with a communicable disease. Keep it neat. Keep it clean. Your attractive appearance in a freshly laundered outfit will not only cheer the patient, but will help to curb the chances of spreading measles or chicken pox to other members of the family. You can also make sure that your "uniform" is infection free by keeping a coverall apron in your patient's room. Wear it only while you are working there. And remember to keep it spotless.

To complete your outfit, wear low-heeled shoes, preferably with rubber soles. They will be more comfortable for you and insure quiet for the patient. And no jangly jewelry, please. That goes for perfume, too, and long, scratchy fingernails.

YOUR HOUSEHOLD HYGIENE

You can further protect your family's health when one of the members is ill by seeing to it that they have lots of nourishing food and rest. Morale is important, too.

You can also protect their good health by keeping the patient's dishes, silver, towels and laundry separate from the rest of the family's. Wash and store them separately.

The most sanitary way to wash your patient's dishes is to use plenty of soap and very hot water, *rub hard,* and rinse well. In some cases the doctor will ask you to wash the patient's dishes with boiling water—that is, to sterilize them.

When you clean a pail or floor or bathroom fixture which infectious matter has touched, use strong cleansers and disinfectants. Your mother will explain how to use these, or follow directions on the bottle or container. (If you have them at hand, wear rubber gloves to protect yourself. Then wash the gloves thoroughly when finished.)

Dispose of infectious materials, such as used bandages, in throw-away paper bags. You and your family's care and thoughtfulness in such matters, whether they appear big or small, will protect each member's health and happiness.

IF MOTHER IS NOT AT HOME

What if your mother is away from home for several days when a member of your family gets sick? Or suppose it's your mother who is sick? Then the best thing for you to do is to get help, if possible.

You'd be surprised how many people there are who can help you in an emergency. The doctor may advise you to get a registered nurse, or a practical nurse. Or a visiting nurse may be all the nursing help you'll need. Her charge is moderate, and is scaled to what your family can afford to pay. When necessary, her services are free of charge.

A part-time housekeeper or a baby sitter can also help you maintain the health and well-being of your family. Of course you will work along with these nurses and helpers all you can.

If you can't get any of these professional helpers, perhaps a relative or neighbor can come to help. But be sure in every case to ask your mother and father for their advice and permission first!

CHERRY SAYS

1. Why is it important, when someone at your house is sick, for every family member to help with household chores?
2. What can *you* do to help care for the patient?
3. How can a home nurse stay well?
4. How can a home nurse keep her family healthy?
5. How can you avoid carrying infection between your patient and the rest of your family?
6. If your mother is not at home when illness strikes, what outside help can you get?

CHAPTER XV

Your Duties as a Home Nurse

"WHAT CAN I DO FIRST?"

BY NOW THE DOCTOR HAS VISITED YOUR PATIENT. You have put the patient to bed promptly. You have had the doctor's prescriptions filled at a reputable pharmacy. One of the first things you can do is to carry out his orders.

Be sure to follow the doctor's instructions *exactly*. If, for instance, he prescribes medicine for the patient at noon, four, eight, and midnight, it must be given exactly on time, or the drug will not have the right effect. Don't give (or take) any medicine unless the doctor has said to, and unless your parents are present.

MORE THAN MEDICINE

Your patient needs a great deal more than just medicine and treatment in order to get well quickly.

He or she needs efficient, tender care. That includes a great many essentials.

Your mother may not have time to perform the dozens of services a sick person requires. She may not have time (nor the unlimited strength) to give the patient nearly continuous attention, and keep the rest of the family healthy at the same time. It is in regard to these essential services that you can be especially helpful. But of course you must know how.

YOUR PATIENT'S BED

Your patient needs a bed which is clean and comfortable. Small discomforts like a lumpy, or too-soft, mattress, wrinkled sheets, or covers which feel too tight or too heavy can make the patient restless and tired. A sick person needs lots of sleep to get well, so make him comfortable.

Sometimes one or two wide boards—such as the extra leaves for your dining table—can be placed underneath the mattress. This is a good way to counteract sagging springs or a mattress which isn't firm. Be sure you cover the mattress with a soft cotton, washable mattress pad.

Change the bed linens as soon as they become limp and mussed, much less soiled. Fresh linens, especially fresh pillowcases, are a must. Remember, too, to turn your patient's pillow over every few hours, so that he rests against its cool side.

Clean, soft, lightweight blankets, and enough of them, are another must. A simple, washable blanket cover of lightweight seersucker or muslin can then be used to protect the blanket and to insure maximum comfort and neatness.

HOW TO MAKE A BED

Every good nurse knows how to make a bed perfectly and quickly. Save yourself steps by making first one side of the bed, then the other side.

1. Place the bottom sheet lengthwise on the bed, centering it. To anchor it, tuck in 12 to 18 inches of sheet under the head of the mattress. Now make a hospital corner (see illustration) then tuck in sheet all along side.

2. Now place the top sheet lengthwise on the bed, and center it. Allow enough at the headboard to fold back 12 to 18 inches of sheet over the blankets, near the patient's face. Allow a 12- to 18-inch margin of top sheet at the foot of the bed, but let it hang loose until you can tuck it in with the blanket.

3. Now place the blanket over the top sheet, about a foot from the head of the bed. Let it hang loose.

4. Circle to the other side of the bed. Tuck the bottom sheet under the head of the mattress, and anchor it by making a corner.

5. Now—important!—grip or pull the bottom sheet toward you until it is taut and perfectly smooth, and tuck it securely under the mattress. Do this three or four times all the way down this side of the bed.

6. At the foot of the bed, tuck the top sheet and blanket *loosely* under the mattress. Tuck them in loosely at the corners, too.

7. Finally, spread the blanket cover over the blanket. Fold the top sheet back over both the blanket

and cover. Put pillowcases on the pillows, and arrange them neatly.

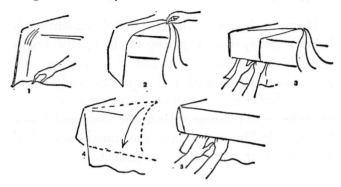

Hospital Corner
1. Grasp edge of sheet about 1 ft. from corner.
2. Lift sheet to form right angle to mattress.
3. Tuck in bottom part of sheet.
4. Drop point of sheet down over side of mattress.
5. Tuck in sheet all along side.

HOW TO USE A DRAWSHEET

Sometimes, when a bedpan is used or sponge baths given, it's a good idea to use a drawsheet to protect the bed and your patient's comfort. The main protection comes from a wide strip or sheet of rubber or pliofilm (or even oilcloth), which you stretch across the bottom sheet under the patient from his head to his knees. Tuck this under the mattress. Cover the rubber strip with the drawsheet, which is a folded sheet. The drawsheet can be slipped out easily and replaced with a fresh one, as needed. Sometimes only the linen drawsheet is all you'll need.

Put on the drawsheet, and the rubber strip if you use it, when you are making the bed. Tuck in tightly.

BED MAKING WITH THE PATIENT IN BED

If your patient is too ill to get out of bed while it is being remade, there is a way to change the linens with the sick person in it. But if I were you, I'd leave that complicated technique to adults—say, your mother or a visiting nurse. However, if you move carefully, don't bump against the bed, and know how to help him to turn, you can *straighten* the bed linens without disturbing your patient.

IMPORTANT: SLEEP

We've talked at length about a comfortable bed, because rest and sleep are great healers. Often extra sleep is all a patient needs to throw off the beginning of an illness. Sleep also acts as "an ounce of prevention."

One summer, when I was nurse at Camp Blue Water for girls, Dr. Lowell and his wife, Janet, and I had a young patient with some alarming symptoms. Sally, aged twelve, was brought to the camp's log cabin infirmary by her counselor, flushed and heavy-eyed. Sally admitted to sore throat, headache, nausea, runny nose, and when I took her temperature it was 100.4 degrees. We put Sally to bed, in isolation, hoping she wouldn't come down with influenza or pneumonia. We *kept* her in bed. We kept her warm and quiet. We gave Sally all the fresh air, liquids, and sleep that one girl could manage.

After three days—I had sat up all one night watching her—Sally announced that she felt fine, and was hungry and demanded a steak. She *was* fine. We had chased away her deep-seated cold infection and prevented flu or pneumonia simply by bed rest—and lots and lots of sleep.

MOVING YOUR PATIENT IN BED

A sick person grows tired and stiff lying too long in the same position. His circulation may grow sluggish unless someone helps him turn on his side or his stomach. But moving him is a job for an adult's strength, perhaps with you helping.

Always tell the patient you are going to move him. Be gentle, don't hurry. If, in being turned, he grows weak or dizzy, pause and let him rest.

In some cases—certain fractures or abdominal wounds—the patient had best not be turned at all.

SUPPORT FOR THE PATIENT IN BED

Another way to ease the sick person in bed, besides moving him, is to support him with pillows. If you have pillows of several shapes and sizes, use them. Or roll up a towel to make a small support.

Here's one comfortable way to use pillows for a patient on his back:

1) Place a bed pillow under the patient's head, as far as his shoulders.

2) Place a foot support, taller than his toes, underneath the covers. This gives him something to brace

himself against and lessens the weight of the blankets on his feet.

3) Bend his knees a little, and place under his knees a small pillow or a folded towel.

TO PROP UP IN BED

If your patient wishes to be propped up for meals or reading, place two bed pillows, lengthwise and overlapping, behind his shoulders. Now place a third bed pillow crosswise under his head. And again, use the foot and knee supports.

TO SIT UP IN BED

When the doctor says your patient may now sit up in bed, you can be ready with a back rest. Place it slanting toward your patient at a comfortable angle. On top of it, adjust three bed pillows, as you would for propping up. Again, use the foot and knee supports. Your patient will also appreciate a pillow at either side of him for an arm support.

HOW TO MAKE A BED REST

Back rests may be purchased, or you can easily improvise one. Use a firm overstuffed cushion from the sofa or from a big chair. Or tie a pillow across a large washboard. A folded card table, slanted against the head of the bed and covered with pillows, or even a tilted chair back, will also serve temporarily. You or your father or brother might make a back rest by taking a sturdy cardboard carton, slitting two of its sides, and refolding it into a large, solid triangle.

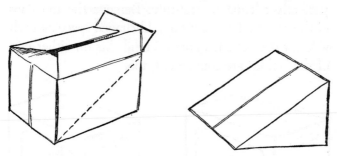

To make bed rest, cut diagonally across each side of carton. Remove pieces. Fold back end of carton shown in picture. Then remove top flaps along creases.

HOW TO MAKE BED COMFORTS

Here are a number of ways to relieve pressure:

Place a soft, folded towel or a small bone-shaped pillow behind the patient's neck for added support and comfort.

A ring, or "doughnut," under elbow, heel, or ear relieves pressure and can help to prevent bedsores. To make a ring, roll a clean stocking down into a "doughnut" and stuff it with cotton.

During a prolonged illness, a purchased rubber air ring or cushion under the hips helps to relieve spinal pressure. For extra comfort and coolness, slip it into a pillowcase.

HOW TO MAKE A BED TABLE

If your patient can sit up for meals, or to read or write letters, he or she will be much more comfortable with a bed table at hand. You don't have one? Well, a heavy cardboard carton can be made over into a perfectly adequate substitute. Remove the top flaps of the carton. Then cut out a U-shaped space on each side for the patient's knees. Hand slits on either end of the "table" are convenient, too.

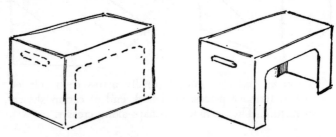

To make bed table, cut out knee hole on each side of sturdy cardboard carton. Make slits at ends for easy lifting.

HELPING YOUR PATIENT IN AND OUT OF BED

The doctor will tell you how soon your patient may get out of bed, and for how long at a time.

You'll need a comfortable, steady chair. Bring it close to the bed, brace it, and drape an open blanket over it. Place pillows as a back support. A footstool is also a handy item. But keep it out of the way until the patient is seated in the chair.

Bring your patient's bathrobe, socks or stockings, slippers and, if needed, an extra blanket or sweater.

While you are getting all these things ready, your mother or the nurse or some other adult helps the patient to a sitting position, swings his legs over the side of the bed, and then puts his extra garments on him. All of this should be done gently and without hurry. If the patient feels weak or dizzy, pause and let him rest; keep him covered so he won't become chilled. Now, with the patient on his feet, he is supported to the chair and helped to sit down. Wrap the open blanket around him, and arrange pillows and footstool comfortably.

Now is your chance to air the bed, tighten the sheets and fluff up the pillows. Your patient will doubly appreciate this after his exciting excursion.

Watch your patient while he is up. If he appears to grow tired or chilled, you and your mother should help him back to bed without delay.

ALL ABOUT THE SICKROOM

A quiet, sunny room, airy but not drafty, at a comfortable temperature, is best for the patient. It should be away from the kitchen and any cooking odors. If the sickroom is near the bathroom, that will save the home nurse many steps.

You'll want to keep the sickroom clean, cheerful, softly lighted, and orderly. It's a good plan to remove any extra clutter, so that your nursing work can be well organized. A bedside table or bureau will hold medicines, clean spoons, a clean glass, and disposable paper tissues. Keep a call bell, fresh drinking water and a glass on a tray at the patient's bedside.

Handy extra items for a home nurse to have are a thermos bottle, flashlight and, for hot wet dressings, a small electric stove.

QUIET, PLEASE

You can help a great deal by keeping the younger children quiet. You can ask your father to muffle the doorbell and telephone bell to a softer ring, and rid the sickroom of any small persistent noises, like a creaking door. You yourself can move quietly, and talk softly and sparingly in the sickroom. It's considerate not to talk to the sick person while he is eating, or bother him in any way. Do not sit on his bed, or bump against it.

DAILY NURSING ROUTINE

If you organize your nursing work and keep to a schedule, then you'll get done—smoothly and efficiently—the dozens of services a patient requires. The other members of your family can help you and your mother set up a routine. Probably you already do some of the following:

1. Collect beforehand everything you will need to give a treatment or serve a meal. If you give the same treatment often, keep the materials together on a tray.
2. Clear away used articles, and wash them or dispose of them promptly. Store every article in its usual place, so you can find it easily when you need it again.
3. Follow a regular daily schedule. In hospitals, we find it helps to write out a list of the things we must do each day, and then arrange these tasks in the most convenient order. We then post the daily schedule where everyone can see it. It helps, too, to write out from day to day a list of special things you'll need to do that day.

4. In planning your schedule, allot yourself the necessary amount of time for each task. Then be on time.
5. Do the most important jobs first. If there just isn't time to do everything, decide what things are unimportant enough to do some other time, or leave them out altogether.

YOUR PATIENT'S CARE

Your daily nursing routine, for example, might look something like this—depending, of course, upon the needs of the individual patient:

1. Morning care of patient
2. Breakfast for patient
3. Bed bath and grooming
4. Take temperature, pulse, and respiration
5. Following the doctor's instructions, give medicines and treatments
6. Straighten and clean sickroom
7. Midmorning nourishment, if doctor permits
8. Rest period for patient
9. Lunch for patient
10. Nap or rest period for patient
11. Midafternoon nourishment, if doctor permits
12. Visitors, if doctor permits. For a convalescent patient, some light recreation
13. Sickroom straightened, and patient freshened up for supper
14. Supper for patient
15. Evening care of patient, and arrange him for the night

That's quite a lot for your mother to do, isn't it—besides keeping your household running as usual and the rest of your family well and cheerful! It takes cooperation by all the members of the family, and it takes practice on your part. Even your mother, even nurses, had to learn all the things that they can now do as if by second nature. I'm sure, if you really try —even in small emergencies—that you can become a first-rate home nurse. Then, when you are grown-up, you'll have a head start on the essential job of being a wife and mother.

CHERRY SAYS

1. What does your patient need, besides medicine and treatment, to get well quickly?
2. Why is it so important for your patient to have a comfortable bed? Can you make a tidy bed?
3. What is a drawsheet?
4. How do you arrange pillows to support a sick person in bed?
5. When the doctor says your patient may get out of bed and sit up in a chair, how can you help him?
6. How can you keep your house and the sickroom quiet for the patient?
7. What is the value of a daily nursing routine?

~~~~~~

CHAPTER XVI

Sickroom Techniques

GIVING TREATMENTS

ONE OF THE FIRST ASSIGNMENTS THE DOCTOR WILL want the home nurse to do is to give the patient simple treatments. If you are willing and have good judgment, your mother may let you assist in this. Or, after you've had some experience at it, your mother may let you give treatment by yourself.

A treatment may mean rubbing a medicated salve on the patient's chest and covering the chest with warm, clean flannel. Or it may consist of applying a hot or cold compress, moist or dry, to an affected part. Or a treatment may be a gargle for your patient, or cleansing and re-bandaging a wound such as an infected toe. We've already discussed these techniques, and many others, in the First Aid section of our book.

First and always—wash your hands with soap and hot water before you give a treatment.

When you stand close to the patient, don't breathe

in his face. And, if he has an infectious illness, turn your face away from his while you work.

TEMPERATURE IS A SIGNAL

A person's temperature is a sign of normal health or of illness. An abnormally high temperature (fever) or an unusually low temperature tells the doctor that something is out of order in the patient's body. That's why it's important to keep a thermometer in your family medicine cabinet in the bathroom. When any family member does not feel or look well, take his temperature right away as a first step. If it rises by more than two or three degrees from normal—which is about 98.6 degrees Fahrenheit—you may decide to telephone the doctor, and at least consult him.

A child's temperature can rise rapidly to a high degree for a short period of time without too much cause for alarm. Keep an eye on the small fry, however. If the temperature continues to be high or if other symptoms of illness develop, then do call your doctor.

When you nurse a patient at home, take his temperature once or twice a day, at the same time each day, or as often as the doctor tells you to.

If your patient's condition should suddenly change —a chill or pain—be sure to take his temperature.

A FEVER THERMOMETER

Do you know how to use a thermometer? You know, of course, that this glass tube is breakable and fragile, so keep it in its case when not in use. Keep it away from heat. Before and after using it, wash the thermometer with soap and cool water, or in an antiseptic solution. Then rinse in cool water.

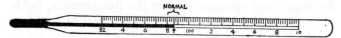

A person's normal temperature is usually 98.6° F.

Look at the diagram and you'll see how to read a thermometer. A dark streak of silver-colored mercury in the tip or bulb will rise to the degree of the patient's temperature. The heat of the patient's body causes this action. To read the thermometer, hold it up against the light and look along the sharper edge between the numbers and the lines. If you don't see the reading at once, keep turning the thermometer ever so slightly until you do. Handle the thermometer delicately; otherwise, you will move the mercury around and alter—falsify—the reading.

There are three ways to take temperature: by mouth, armpit, and rectum. Doctors and nurses use the latter two methods for infants or for patients who have special disabilities. You will take temperature by mouth. Be sure to leave the thermometer under the patient's tongue for at least three minutes to obtain an accurate reading.

HOW TO TAKE TEMPERATURE

1. Have your patient sit or lie down.
2. Hold the thermometer firmly by the top (not by its silvery bulb).
3. Shake the thermometer with a loose movement of your wrist. This is to lower the mercury to 95° F or

below. Stand away from the furniture while you do this, to avoid hitting and breaking the thermometer.

4. Place the bulb under the patient's tongue, a little to one side.
5. After three minutes, remove the thermometer, holding it by the top end. Wipe off any moisture with a clean cloth or paper.
6. Read the thermometer. Write down your reading on your medical record.
7. Wash the thermometer at once, and return it to its case.

HOW TO TAKE YOUR PATIENT'S PULSE

A person's pulse tells you how many heart beats there are per minute, as the heart pumps the blood through the body. If a pulse is much too fast or too slow, that is a signal to the doctor.

Have your patient sit or lie down, with his hand and wrist resting in a comfortable position. Place your forefingers (never your thumb) on the inside of his wrist. Can you feel the pulse in the veins? Now, consult your watch, and for one full minute count the pulse beats. Or, if you have a watch with a sweep second hand, you can take your patient's pulse for a quarter of a minute; then just multiply by four for the correct count. Have it? Fine. Now just jot down in your medical record your patient's pulse rate, the hour, date, and any marked irregularity.

What is a normal rate of pulse? It can vary a good deal, depending on the person. To begin with, it is different for men, women and children. Usually the pulse rate for men is about 65 to 70 beats a minute.

It is about 75 to 80 beats for women, while a child's pulse beat is faster. From ages six to twelve, it is about 90 to 105; in the teens, it reaches adult rate.

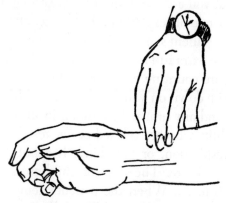

To take patient's pulse, place fingers, not thumb, on wrist. Count beats for 1 minute.

Tall people usually have a slower pulse rate than short people. Older people usually have a slower pulse rate than young adults. But later the rate quickens again in very old people. Sounds complicated, doesn't it? That is why it is your job to record your patient's pulse, but your doctor's responsibility alone to interpret it.

HOW TO TAKE YOUR PATIENT'S RESPIRATION

Respiration tells you how many breaths per minute your patient takes. If the rate of breathing is much too fast or much too slow, it can be a danger signal. That is why a hospital nurse, and often a home nurse, takes a patient's TPR (temperature, pulse and respiration) daily as part of her nursing routine.

Many patients grow self-conscious if they are aware that you are watching their breathing; this can alter their rate of respiration. Therefore, after having taken the patient's pulse, keep your fingers on his wrist for an extra full minute and do not let him know that you are counting each rise and fall of his chest. Then write down on your medical record his respiration rate and any unusual condition in his breathing.

For adults who are relaxed or "at rest," the usual rate of respiration, or breathing, is about 16 to 20 times per minute. The rate for children is approximately 20 to 25. When the patient's temperature is high, his respiration rate will usually increase, too.

You must also watch for other symptoms besides the respiration rate. If your patient's breathing seems labored, noisy or painful, report this to your doctor.

KEEPING A MEDICAL RECORD FOR THE DOCTOR

The doctor depends on the home nurse to report to him, accurately and in detail, everything concerning the patient's condition, care and behavior. The doctor needs this to help him make and recheck his diagnosis. So you can see that, since the patient's condition changes from day to day, your report is especially important.

It's best to keep a written report, as no one could possibly remember accurately the dozens of details. Also, if you and your mother and perhaps a nurse, or another member of the family, are all taking care of the patient, some of you might get mixed up. Imagine if the patient receives his medicine twice instead of once, or doesn't get it all, because of some confusion! A record will protect the patient from such mistakes. So keep one written report in a notebook.

You'll find it convenient to make a chart for each day, with the date and the necessary headings, with space left open for your entries.

Leave space, too, for the doctor to write his instructions in the record. If he gives instructions by telephone, be sure to enter them in the record right away. And check with him for changes in instructions each time you see him or talk with him.

On page 192, you will find a list of items that the doctor will want recorded and to know about daily. Keep your record brief and exact. (BM means bowel movement; UR, urination.)

Write everything down as soon as it is done.

Keep your medical record out of the patient's sight, if you can, and out of the reach of small children.

If there is any sudden change in your patient's condition—such as a noticeable rise in temperature, pain, bleeding, swelling, rash, or pronounced restlessness—telephone the doctor to report it at once. Then record it on your daily chart.

HOW TO GIVE MEDICINE

Give (or take) medicine only if the doctor has said to, and only if your parents are present.

Give medicine with caution! Read the label. Read

Date & Hour	T	P	R	Diet and Medicine	BM	UR	Remarks
March 1 8:00 A.M.	99.5	74	22		x		Slept most of night.
8:30 A.M.				Breakfast: small glass of orange juice, one soft boiled egg, toast, glass of warm milk			Morning care

Good appetite |
9 A.M.				Medicine #123456 —1 teaspoon			
10 A.M.					x	x	Headache. A little coughing
11 A.M.– noon				Treatment as prescribed			Nap, half hour
12 noon				Lunch: 1 bowl chicken broth with rice, 1 saucer apple sauce and 2 sugar cookies			
1 P.M.				Medicine #7890 —1 tablet			Coughing less. Headache gone
2–3 P.M.						x	Bed rest, reading
4 P.M.	100	76	24	One cup of hot tea			
4:30–5:30 P.M.						x	Nap, one hour
6 P.M.				Supper: one lamb chop, boiled potato, spinach, baked apple, glass of milk			
7:30 P.M.						x	Evening care
8 P.M.							Asleep

the doctor's instructions. Give the exact amount prescribed. Give it at the time prescribed. Give it only to the person for whom the doctor prescribed it.

If you ever should happen to make a mistake in giving medicine, report the mistake at once to your doctor. But no mistakes, please! Be careful.

When you give *liquid medicine:*

1. Shake the medicine bottle well.

2. Give only as much medicine as it called for. Pour the medicine into a measuring spoon, or measure it into a medicine glass.

3. If drops are given, use a medicine dropper and count the drops aloud.

4. Be sure your patient swallows the medicine.

5. Give him a drink of water, if allowed.

When you give *medicine as powder or tablets:*

1. These may be dissolved in water, or placed well back on the patient's tongue.

2. Offer your patient a glass of water. If he throws his head back while he swallows, the tablet usually will roll down easily.

"NASTY-TASTING STUFF!"

No one enjoys the disagreeable taste of certain medicines. You can counteract this, however, by giving your patient a small glass of orange juice, a cookie or cracker, or some fruit immediately after the medicine—*if* the doctor has no objection. Or you can disguise the medicine's taste by mixing it with some appealing food or liquid. One very small boy who was my patient loved "orange soda"—which consisted of a glass of orange juice mixed with a half teaspoon of castor oil and dab of vanilla ice cream.

GIVING MEDICINE TO CHILDREN

If a child balks about taking his medicine, a good nurse does not force or bribe him. Instead, she explains that the medicine will help him get well. She explains that his parents and the doctor will be proud of him if he cooperates and takes his medicine.

It's easier, though, to talk to the child about something he's interested in and, while his attention is distracted, slip the medicine into him. Be quick and be matter-of-fact, so that it won't even occur to him to object.

A pill or tablet is hard for a child to swallow. Crush and mix it with a little pleasant-tasting food like applesauce or jam. Or put the crushed tablet in something lumpy and soft, like banana, and follow it with a pleasant-tasting drink.

If you put medicine in a child's milk or orange juice, the unaccustomed flavor may spoil his taste for a once favorite food. Try some other fruit juice whose flavor is new to him.

HOW TO FILL A HOT WATER BAG

When the doctor orders "a hot dry application," you will fill a rubber hot water bag. There is a little more to doing this correctly than you might think. A too hot bag can burn or scorch the patient. A too full bag, resting on or against the patient, is an uncomfortable weight. The bag also must not leak and must be perfectly dry.

Here is the correct way to fill it:

1. Test the water with your fingers. It should be hot, not scalding.

2. Fill the bag only one-third to one-half full.

3. Lay the bag down, holding up the open end, and press the bag gently to expel the air. This makes the bag pliable. Now screw in the stopper firmly.

4. Dry the bag thoroughly. Then hold it upside down to make sure that it doesn't leak.

Some patients like to have a towel cover around the hot water bag. If you don't have one on hand, a fresh dish towel makes an excellent substitute. Fasten the towel in position with safety pins, but be sure not to pin the towel to the bag! And remember— refill the bag when it loses heat.

If you have no hot water bottle, a large heated plate or a jar of hot water, securely sealed and dried, are fair substitutes.

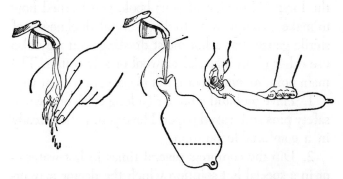

To prepare hot water bag, test water for hot, not scalding, temperature. Fill bag ⅓ to ½ full. Now, holding open end up, press out excess air. Screw on cap tightly.

HOW TO PREPARE AN ICE BAG

An ice bag is used for dry cold applications.

You probably have seen round ice bags, made of rubber, for general use. There are also long narrow ice bags to fasten around a sore throat, if prescribed.

How do you fill an ice bag? First crush the ice into small pieces. Run the pieces under cold water to melt away any sharp edges. Then fill the bag only half full and expel air. If you wish, cover the bag with a small towel. Then apply.

A substitute for an ice bag may be a hot water bottle filled with ice water. Or you can fill a rubber bathing cap with crushed ice; but remember to tie the cap closed very securely.

HOW TO PREPARE A HOT MOIST COMPRESS

In our discussion of compresses and bandages, in the First Aid section of your book, you learned how to make a compress by folding several thicknesses of sterile gauze. For a hot moist dressing, you may also use other clean material of wool or soft cotton. The main point to remember is not to get your patient wet.

1. Have on hand a binder (a long cloth or towel), safety pins and waxed paper. Have your patient ready in a comfortable position.

2. Dip the compress several times in hot water— or in a special hot solution which the doctor may order. Wring it out dry.

3. Shake out the compress to release the steam.

4. Apply the compress gradually to the patient's affected area.

5. Cover the compress with the waxed paper, then with the binder, and secure the binder with safety pins. But be sure that the pinned application is snug, not tight, fitting.

You'll want to keep the hot compress hot. A hot water bottle helps. However, it's usually better to apply a fresh hot compress about every twenty minutes, as needed.

HOW TO PREPARE A COLD MOIST COMPRESS

Soak your compress in cold water or ice water, and wring it out dry. Apply gradually to the inflamed area. You will not need a binder. When it grows warm, replace it with a fresh compress, about every three minutes. And careful! Keep your patient dry, warm and comfortable.

ASSISTING YOUR MOTHER OR A NURSE

Even if you do not give treatments or medication by yourself, you can give important assistance in several ways. One way is to assemble and have ready for your mother, the nurse, or the doctor, all the articles they will need. Another way to help is by knowing what to do and how to do it, so that you stand ready and trained to be of assistance. It may be a seemingly small matter: handing your mother a sterile dressing, properly prepared, at exactly the moment she needs it for the patient; or keeping the daily medical chart completely and accurately filled out. Except that these aren't small matters at all!

CHERRY SAYS

1. How do you take a temperature?
2. How do you take a pulse? Respiration?
3. What should you include in your daily medical record for the doctor?
4. How do you give liquid medicine? Pills or capsules?
5. How can you make medicine more palatable?
6. How do you fill a hot water bag? An ice bag?
7. How do you prepare a hot moist compress? A cold moist compress?

~~~~~~

CHAPTER XVII

Your Patient's Comfort

SICKROOM HYGIENE

WHEN I WAS JUST STARTING OUT AS A STUDENT nurse, it seemed to me that I was forever washing or sterilizing everything I touched and forever washing my hands. By now it's second nature to do so. Cleanliness is a safety measure and a powerful weapon against illness, especially against contagious disease.

Don't you agree that cleanliness is a small price to pay for good health? We all want to be immaculate personally and live in clean rooms as a matter of fastidiousness as well.

A clean sickroom is a must. Dust carries germs. Air, dust, and mop the floor of the sickroom every morning, quickly and quietly, so that you will not disturb your patient.

Remove *promptly* from the sickroom all soiled bandages, paper tissues, linens, dishes, and leftover food. Keep these away from well persons and from all things the well family members use.

Cover containers of medicine, glasses and spoons with a clean towel. These things must be kept clean. They are not much fun to look at anyway.

Protect sickroom furniture and floors with clean newspapers. Use disposable paper towels, napkins, cups and plates.

Use disposable paper tissues rather than cloth handkerchiefs. Keep a box of paper tissues and a large paper or cardboard wastebasket close and handy to the patient's bedside.

When you handle contaminated matter in the sickroom, such as soiled dressings or used handkerchiefs, dispose of them in paper bags. Then throw away or burn the paper bag.

HOW TO MAKE A WASTEPAPER BAG

Look at the step-by-step, numbered illustrations. Then read the following instructions, glancing to the diagram for guidance at each step. You'll need a double sheet of newspaper and cellophane tape. Have them? Then we're ready to begin.

1. Place the newspaper flat in front of you, as if you were about to read page one from top to bottom.

2. Take hold of the bottom edge of the pages and fold the newspaper in half horizontally, at the center, as illustrated in diagram No. 2. Keep this center fold facing you.

3. Now take the top edge of the newspaper and, by folding it, bring it down to meet the center fold. This makes a cuff.

4. Turn the newspaper over, with the cuff side down and the smooth side up. Continue to keep the center fold toward you all the time you are making the bag.

5. Fold the newspaper in thirds from both sides. Press down firmly so that the creases will hold the fold.

6. Tuck one side of the cuff into the other side of the cuff. This locks the sides together. Then fasten the joined cuffs with a bit of cellophane tape.

7. Bring the flap down over the locked cuff.

8. Now put your left hand between the top and second pages of the *flap*. Stand the bag up. Spread the sides of the flap open and, with your left hand, reach down to make sure the bag will have a bottom.

9. Shape the bag gently, taking care not to rip it.

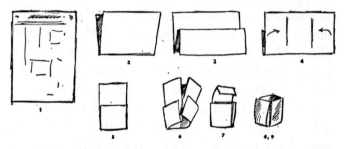

1. To make paper bag, smooth out single sheet of newspaper.
2. Fold paper in half.
3. Fold front flap again in half to make cuff.
4. Turn paper, folding it in thirds.
5. Smooth and flatten edges.
6. Insert one end of folded paper into cuff of other end.
7. Fold top over into cuff.
8. Insert hand into open end to shape bag.

If you wish, you can use the flap to pin the bag to the side of the bedclothes for convenient access. Then when you are ready to dispose of the bag, just flip the flap up and over the opening. This closes the bag and reduces any chance of contagion.

To make a larger bag, just use two double sheets of newspaper, opened to full size—as if you were reading pages two and three.

Heavy brown paper grocery bags can be used, too. But it's more fun to make your own.

For waste material which is too heavy or bulky for a paper bag, use a metal receptacle—for instance, a bucket. After disposal, scrub the bucket.

COMMUNICABLE DISEASE

A patient with a contagious disease must be isolated in a room by himself. Keep the other members of the family away from him—pets, too. And no visitors, please. Probably you, too, had best keep a safe distance away from him. Your best contribution may be helping with other household and family tasks.

However, if you are vaccinated and permitted as a home nurse to go in and out of the sickroom, be careful not to be a "carrier"—not to carry germs in and out with you. You have the double responsibility of protecting your patient from new infection and protecting the well members of your family from contagion.

We've already talked about your wearing a cover-all apron while in the sickroom, and leaving it in the sickroom. Turn your head away, or wear a gauze face mask, while tending your patient.

Wash, wash, wash your hands, before and after caring for the patient. When you leave the sickroom, go directly to the bathroom, being careful not to touch anything on your way. Cover the faucet handle with a clean paper towel and turn on the water. Now throw away the paper towel, and wash your hands thoroughly with soap and hot water.

Quarantine is a very thorough precaution and isolation imposed by your local Board of Health or your doctor. It is necessary in case of such contagious illness as scarlet fever or measles. It is such a complicated procedure that I'll only say here—to quote Mrs. Terrell whose small son, Jimmy, I cared for when I was a visiting nurse—"It's easier to keep well in the first place."

AN OUNCE OF PREVENTION

Even though a disease *may not* be thought communicable, disease germs can be passed along to other people. That's why it is safest to observe every precaution.

KERCHOO!

Don't forget that the common cold is a communicable disease, too. If you cough or sneeze, cover your face with a clean handkerchief or a clean paper tissue. Dispose of these where other people can't be infected by them.

You can expect the same consideration from others. Turn your face away from persons with colds.

PERSONAL CARE AND HYGIENE FOR YOUR PATIENT

An invalid needs help to keep himself or herself clean and comfortably groomed. You can assist him with daily personal care in the following way:

1. Before breakfast, if the patient must stay in bed, bring a tray holding a basin of warm water, soap, wash cloth, and towel. Fill the basin only halfway to avoid spills. Help him to wash his face and hands.

2. Next bring a tray holding his toothbrush, toothpaste or powder, a glass of water, an empty basin, and towel. For a mouthwash, bring also a glass of warm water into which you have stirred one-half teaspoonful each of salt and bicarbonate of soda (baking soda).

3. If the patient can get up and go to the bathroom, a bedpan will not be necessary. But if one must be used, keep it scrupulously clean and use its cover. Warm it first with warm water, and dry it well. The patient can summon you by call bell when ready to have the bedpan taken away. Immediately bring the patient a basin of water, soap, and towel to wash his hands.

4. Give your patient his or her comb and brush, a waste container, and if desired, a hand mirror. Don't forget to bring a nail file occasionally.

5. Have plenty of fresh nightgowns or pajamas on hand for the patient. Keep robe and slippers within

the patient's easy reach. If he or she is permitted to sit up in bed, a bed jacket or sweater will be needed, except in very hot weather.

A BED BATH

This is a sponge bath in bed. It is best left to your mother or a nurse, since it takes considerable skill not to get the bed wet or damp. You can assist, however, by seeing that the sickroom is warm and private, and that warm water, soap, towels, and talcum or deodorant are on hand.

Bring fresh pajamas or gown for the patient to put on after the bed bath. A fresh pillowcase, too, will refresh the invalid.

A BACK RUB

A relaxing back rub is one of the pleasantest attentions you can give your patient. Use rubbing alcohol, though some patients prefer a lightly-scented toilet water. Warm it by holding it in hot water. Be sure your hands are warm, too.

Have your patient lie comfortably on his stomach or side. Pour a little of the rubbing alcohol or toilet water into your hand, then moisten your other hand with it, so that both hands are moist.

With long, smooth, continuous strokes, glide your hands over the patient's back, first all the way up, then all the way down, and repeat. Use a firm, moderate pressure. Finish the back rub with a little talcum.

FEEDING THE PATIENT

To get well quickly, your patient will need plenty of nourishing food. The doctor will give you a list of the foods and beverages your patient requires. If he is unable to feed himself, you can help him. It takes gentleness and patience.

Liquids. At your drugstore you can buy straws and also a glass drinking tube which is bent at a comfortable angle. This tube makes it possible for the patient who cannot sit up to sip liquids, without gulping or spilling. It helps to prop up your patient with pillows, if the doctor allows that. Insert the bent tube in the glass of water or milk or orange juice, and hold the glass steady for your patient while he sips.

For children there are chocolate-flavored straws which are fun with milk.

When you help your patient to drink from a cup, put your hand under his head to support him. Hold the cup in your other hand, and let the patient hold the bottom of the cup, to guide it.

Foods. First, see that your patient is in a comfortable position on the near side of the bed. Have ready on the tray food, silverware, napkins, a glass of water, and anything else you'll need. Be sure that the foods are at a comfortable temperature—warm, but never scalding hot. Bring a chair to the bedside for yourself and a napkin to protect the bedding. Let your patient see what he is going to eat.

Now, going slowly, offer a spoonful at a time. Feed the patient from the side of the spoon, not the tip. Keep the bottom side of the spoon dry to avoid drips and dribbles. Offer small mouthfuls and alternate bites of this or that food. Encourage the patient to eat, but give him plenty of time to swallow and rest. You want him to enjoy his meal to the fullest.

PREPARING THE PATIENT FOR THE NIGHT

After you have completed your last chores of the day—given the patient medicine or treatment and any evening nourishment—then you are ready to make him comfortable for a good night's rest.

Here are the steps to follow:

1. Bathroom or bedpan
2. Wash patient's face and hands
3. Comb patient's hair
4. Help him brush his teeth
5. Change nightgown if desired, and bring a bed-jacket if needed
6. Bring an extra blanket, if needed
7. Fluff up the bed pillows, and arrange them for support
8. If your patient needs or wants a night light, arrange a dim light at his bedside. See that it doesn't shine in his eyes. Or give him a flashlight
9. Leave fresh drinking water and a call bell on his bedside table
10. Adjust the windows for fresh air, without direct drafts on the patient

Finally, ask the patient if he is comfortable and if there is anything else he wants. Cheerfully reassure him that members of the family are nearby, and wish him a very good night.

CHERRY SAYS

1. How do you keep a sickroom clean?
2. Can you make a wastepaper bag?
3. How does a home nurse avoid being a carrier of contagion?
4. How do you help a patient to keep clean and comfortable?
5. Describe how you would give a back rub.
6. How do you feed a helpless patient?
7. How do you make a patient ready for the night?

~~~~~~~~~~~~~~~~~~~~~~~~~~~~~~~~~~~~~~

CHAPTER XVIII

Tips for a Cheerful Sickroom

AS EVERY NURSE KNOWS, THERE IS A GREAT DEAL more to nursing than merely meeting your patient's physical needs. You must help a sick person to feel cheerful, so that he or she will *want* to get well quickly. Good morale is half the battle.

WINKY'S CASE

Once, as you read earlier under Burns, I had as a hospital patient a little boy, Winky, whose face was badly burned in a home accident. Winky's father was frightened that he would be disfigured. This frightened Winky so much that we could scarcely get the child to eat or sleep. He was not going to withstand shock from the burn and surgery in that state of mind, no matter what miracles the plastic surgeon performed.

So I explained to Winky that he was going to look

just as he had before, told him stories while he had his feedings, and held his hand while he drifted off to sleep. We also managed to set up a bedside radio and a miniature Christmas tree, which cheered him greatly. Winky, with me wheeling him in a chair, became the most popular guest at all the ward Christmas parties. And he recovered by leaps and bounds.

A young person can make a fine contribution to a patient's welfare by keeping cheerful. It is here that you can help especially.

MM, DELICIOUS!

Everybody enjoys good things to eat. But appetizing meals are particularly important to the invalid. Attractive meals are welcome breaks in the course of a long day. Your patient's interest in food should be encouraged in any case, for a well-balanced diet will contribute heavily to his speedy recovery.

Serve your patient's meals on time. A person who is weak and hungry should not be kept waiting. Just before you bring his tray, see that his hands and face are washed and that he is comfortably supported by pillows.

Serve him small portions. Small portions appear more appetizing to a sick person, and he can always have seconds. And since some patients need to be encouraged to eat, present all trays with a smile and a good word for the meal's menu.

It isn't necessary to insist that your patient consume the last morsel. If he doesn't like what you have served him, don't force him to eat it. Find a substitute, perhaps a favorite of his, among the foods which the doctor has said the patient may have.

You'll be surprised, though, how often patients have a hearty appetite, even with lack of exercise. A good appetite is a good sign of recovery.

If your patient is able to feed himself, it's usually best to leave him alone with his tray. Of course you will be within call. And when you come back to clear away the tray and dishes, be quick and quiet.

AN ATTRACTIVE TRAY

In Chapter (XV) we talked about how to make a bed table out of a cardboard carton. This fits across the patient's lap. By placing your tray of food on it, you keep the weight off the patient. It's steadier that way, too.

How good are you at arranging an attractive tray? For the sick person who never wants to hear of food again, a glass of milk in a ruby-red tumbler and bread-and-butter finger-strips arranged like a lattice may surprise and tempt him into eating. There are colorful paper napkins and inexpensive colored or patterned china to lend extra variety to a sickroom tray. Surprises like a flower, a funny greeting card, a perfect red apple, or an interesting newspaper clipping on his tray can cheer up and delight a person confined to bed. Or try putting a small new toy on a child's tray. And remember that small fry enjoy cookies, or even bread-and-butter, cut in animal shapes.

The food itself on your patient's tray should have variety of color and texture. For example, don't serve all-white meals: creamed chicken, mashed potatoes, and cauliflower. That's three soft white foods and rather monotonous, don't you think? Imagine a more tempting combination: on the creamed chicken, a sprinkle of red paprika, or red pimento, and minced green parsley; a crisp brown baked potato; chewy yellow carrot rings. Isn't that livelier?

An attractive tray of appetizing food
holds much appeal for the convalescent.

You can be of particular help to your mother by setting the patient's tray. Remember the rest of the household, too—you can set and clear the table.

TEMPTING AND NOURISHING

For good health, you and your family should have a portion of these seven basic foods every day: bread and cereals; butter or margarine; yellow or green, leafy vegetables; citrus fruits such as oranges, grapefruit; potatoes and other vegetables and fruits; for protein, meat or poultry or fish or eggs or dried peas and beans; milk, cheese, or ice cream.

Good menus for your patient will include the seven basic foods every day, depending on the doctor's diet orders. Follow the diet he prescribes. Sometimes the patient may have many or all of the same foods the family is having. He may temporarily lose his taste for sweet foods.

Remember to write on the medical record the kinds and amounts of food that your patient eats daily. This is important information which the doctor needs.

A convalescent especially needs plenty of nourishing food to build him up after an illness. So here are a few suggestions for between-meal "extras" or surprises: ginger ale, bouillon with crackers, milk shake, eggnog, fruit, fruit juice, milk, and ice cream. Don't you think a strawberry sundae—vanilla ice cream topped with fresh-frozen strawberries—would cheer up any patient?

To help relieve your mother, you might be the one who prepares the patient's snacks—and even his breakfast or lunch.

PLEASANT SURROUNDINGS

Imagine if you felt sick and weak and had to stay in bed, in the same room, day after day. But now imagine green plants brightening the sickroom. Imagine a mobile, cut out of colored paper, lazily turning at the foot of your bed, or a bouquet of flowers, fresh from the garden, gracing your bedside table. Feel better already, don't you?

You probably know how to start a sweet potato plant: simply put a sweet potato in a good-sized jar or bottle of water so that half of the potato is immersed. You don't want the potato to rest against the bottom of the jar, so prop your plant-to-be up with tooth picks at the top edge of the jar. Soon green sprouts will appear, then leaves. And any patient will be interested. (My mother says, "A growing, living plant is a companion.") Once, when I was sick, a bowl of brilliant goldfish kept me entertained for days.

A sweet potato, suspended by toothpicks in a jar of water, makes an attractive sickroom plant.

Have you ever made a ribbon mobile of get-well cards? Hang it from a light fixture or from the ceiling above the foot of the patient's bed. It's something colorful and moving for him to watch.

Small attentions add to a cheerful room. If your patient's bed is high, bring a box as an easy step down. Older persons, who feel the cold, appreciate extra heat in the sickroom or extra bedjackets and bed socks. If your patient has within easy reach familiar things which he likes and needs, he will feel more self-reliant—and more eager to get well quickly.

Hospitals now paint their wards and private rooms in soft, pleasing colors and hang draperies of colorful fabrics at the windows. This, too, contributes to good morale and helps the patient to recover quickly. Is your patient's sickroom cheerful? See if you can think of ways to introduce pleasing, muted colors or soft lighting or even a more comfortable arrangement of the furniture.

You can do this by drawing a floor plan of your patient's room. You will need a piece of graph paper with ¼-inch squares. Each square represents one foot in the room's measurements. After marking off the room on the graph, indicate the location of windows and doors. Now draw cutouts of the furniture and lamps, again allowing ¼ inch for each foot. Arrange the cutouts in different ways on the floor plan. While you keep in mind good ventilation and lighting, see if you can work out a more cheerful room. (This is the way decorators do it, and it is called making a templet.)

PLEASANT THINGS TO DO

Your patient needs diversions to relieve the monotony of his long day and to perk up his interest in getting well. These diversions should not tax his strength and must not last too long at a time. If you are in any doubt, consult the doctor. Don't force entertainment on your patient, but on the other hand, sick people have a tendency to be gloomy and may need a little coaxing. They really need cheering up on your part.

You as a young person may be just the right companion. We've found in hospitals that teen-age nurses' aides are like a tonic for our patients' morale. Natu-

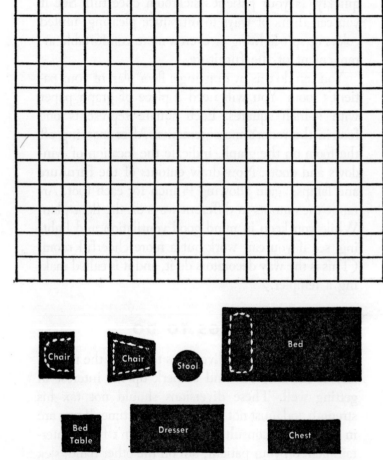

Each templet square represents 1 ft. of your room's dimensions. Measure room. Then outline its measurements on templet. Trace furniture on paper for silhouette cutouts.

rally you will continue to be gentle and quiet in the sickroom, and plan diversions which suit your patient's condition.

Some activities, like reading or solitaire, allow the patient to amuse himself, in bed or seated in a chair. It's good for an invalid to be independent; it encourages him, as a step in getting well. You can help by bringing books from the public library and magazines which he'll like. Today's newspaper brings him in touch with the outside world. A good reading lamp is a must, with the switch within the patient's reach.

A radio on the bedside table is generally welcome, too, but it should be used with moderation. If you can hang a mirror so that it reflects the street and outdoors, that will interest your patient, too.

Does your patient have a hobby? Knitting materials could be set up on a bridge table, next to a comfortable chair and hassock or footstool. You might plan a desk arrangement for letter writing. Or perhaps your patient likes to make things. Collecting items for a scrapbook, sewing, or arts and crafts take an invalid's mind off his or her illness.

For children, you'll think up all sorts of things to do from practicing magic tricks to making whimsical figures out of pipe cleaners and clothespins. Now is the time a child can learn how to knit or to load and operate a camera. Look around your house for toys that have been put away and half forgotten, and for old family snapshots which have stories to go along with them. Children, and some grownups, too, will enjoy your reading aloud to them.

Elderly persons and those who have chronic illnesses want to feel needed and useful, in spite of their physical handicaps. See if you can find light, useful tasks for them, such as shelling peas or sewing on buttons or looking up a number in the telephone directory or helping address envelopes for some community drive. Be tactful. Give them a chance to do things for other people.

Games are fun for patients of all ages. An invalid may enjoy crossword puzzles, a jigsaw puzzle, or card games. Games for him and one or two other persons provide companionship. Not more than three persons all at once, please; otherwise the game and the conversation will become too strenuous for an invalid or a convalescent. Here are some games you and the patient and perhaps a third person could play: Ghost (and other word games), checkers or chess, Authors, Old Maid, Monopoly, Alphabetical Cities, rummy, Russian Bank.

Did you ever make a "surprise box," or did anyone ever give you one? This is how it's done. Collect a number of small, inexpensive gifts, mostly from the five-and-ten-cent store. Wrap each gift separately in bright paper and mark on it the hour when the patient may open his "surprise"—before taking his four o'clock medicine, for instance, or just after his regular nap time. Put all the wrapped gifts in a box or plastic bag. Children enjoy these surprises a great deal.

A pleasant way to break the patient's day is with personal attentions. Hair brushing, a back rub with toilet water, frequent washing of the patient's face and hands—these are all refreshing. A feminine patient will also appreciate a ribbon for her hair, and will feel 100 per cent better in her best nightgown and bedjacket.

If the doctor permits them, light between-meals refreshments—bouillon at 10:30 A.M., fruit juice at 3 P.M.—are another nice way to lighten the patient's day. It will save Mother steps, and possibly let *her* take a nap, if you take charge of these refreshments.

TWO WORDS OF CAUTION

Don't overtire your patient, or he may not be able to sleep at night. Schedule regular nap times. Then, on schedule, darken the room and leave the patient alone to rest or sleep.

Don't spoil or overindulge your patient. A little humoring is enough. If he or she has a highly enjoyable time being an invalid, with every whim catered to, he may delay getting well.

VISITORS

Did you ever stop to think that being ill is a lonesome business? Suddenly your patient is cut off from family and friends, and marooned in the sickroom. When he begins to recover, he'll want to see people. First of all, he'll want to see members of the family. (Perhaps he can join the family at meals.) As he grows stronger, he'll be glad to see friends.

Having visitors in is a good way to boost the patient's morale. When he hears about the activities he is missing, he'll want to get well quickly. Unless there is a contagious disease, you should encourage companionship. The doctor will tell you when your patient is strong enough to entertain visitors.

It is usually advisable to keep the visits short so as not to tire the patient. Fifteen minutes may be quite long enough, while half an hour should be the maximum. Before the visitor enters the sickroom you might tell him, privately, that the doctor permits visits only of such-and-such duration. If the visitor overstays, or if the patient urges him to stay, then you can tactfully say that, pleasant as his visit is, now it must end.

During the visit, you might look in to see how your patient is taking it. Make sure the visitor is not noisy or does not tell any disturbing news.

It's a good plan, too, not to permit too many visitors on any one day. And they should not visit while the patient is eating, or having a treatment. The best times for visitors are late in the morning, or after the patient's afternoon nap.

Your own visits to the patient should not be too long. Be cheerful, and don't talk too much. Give the patient a chance to talk, too.

Visitors are fine, but be sure to allow the patient some time for himself.

YOUR OWN ATTITUDE IS IMPORTANT

Attitudes are catching. If you are hopeful, your patient will be encouraged. As a home nurse you'll want to be cheerful, quiet, firm.

Allow for a sick person to be a little cross or unreasonable. Often it's a sign that he is getting well.

A convalescent patient who is nearly well grows restless. Here is where you can use your tact and ingenuity. Find light tasks for him to do, or light activities with the family. Remove from his room all the signs of illness that you can. The sooner the doctor permits him to go outdoors, the better. Just don't let the convalescent patient get overtired.

Praise your patient occasionally for his cooperation. Or compliment him for some good trait.

It isn't enough for you to be skillful in nursing techniques. It's important for you to care for your patient in the right spirit. Be generous, willing, cheerful.

CHERRY SAYS

1. Why is it particularly important to keep your patient cheerful?
2. How can meals aid a sick person's morale?
3. Can you name the seven basic foods?
4. How can a sickroom be made more pleasant?
5. What are good diversions for a sick person?
6. What are the important points for a home nurse to remember about a patient's visitors?
7. Why is your own attitude as a home nurse important?

~~~~~~

CHAPTER XIX

Baby Sitting

TAKING CARE OF CHILDREN

IF SOMEONE IS SICK AT YOUR HOUSE, YOU MIGHT BE delegated to take care of the children. If your mother is away, this might be your job.

Baby sitting is a responsible job. For a few hours you are, in effect, the children's mother. You have sole responsibility for keeping the children safe, well, and happy. To take care of the lives of others—especially small children, who can't look out for themselves—is about as important a job as there is.

The main qualification for taking care of children is to like children and to enjoy being with them. Just think about it from a small child's point of view. Suppose you were small and dependent and not very old—how would *you* like being left alone with someone who wasn't really sympathetic with youngsters? If you have a warm heart and a level head, you can be a good baby sitter.

222

Taking care of children is fun—and it's good training for when you have children of your own.

CARING FOR A SICK CHILD

Occasionally, in your own family or in a neighbor's emergency, you'll be called upon to help take care of a sick child. You'll want to be equally good with children whether they are sick or well. Here are a few points to use when your small charge isn't well:

1. Remember that the child may be in pain, or may be afraid of the doctor or the medicine or the illness itself. Explain to him that there is nothing to be afraid of. Tell him exactly how you are helping him, and reassure him that he will soon feel well again—especially if he cooperates.

2. Crying and restlessness, with babies and very young children, are signals of discomfort or needs. Perhaps a baby is hungry, or thirsty, or his garments are tightly twisted. Perhaps a small child has a stomach ache or a bad dream. Find out what bothers your patient, make him comfortable, and reassure him.

3. If the child is not too ill, find things that will amuse him, even if he must stay in bed. Simple toys or games or story-telling will comfort him. Music, whether it's radio or records (not too loud, please), is a good cheerer-upper, too. Bright-colored, patterned plastic bandages for children help take the sting out of a scraped knee.

4. Good nursing is much the same for children as for grownups, except that you will allow for the

child's age and special needs. Try to keep to his usual schedule. Regular naps are important.

5. Never give a child medicine or any sort of remedy, unless the doctor has said to do so and the child's parents are present.

Did you ever give a small girl a beauty treatment —hair brushing, a new hair style with a ribbon or flower, a manicure? Did you ever bring a small boy an inexpensive magnifying glass or a wooden construction puzzle? A collection of funny papers and cartoons which you have cut out especially for your small patient will do much to brighten his day, too.

HOW TO BE A GOOD SITTER

Let's suppose you arrive some time before the children's parents go out for the evening. Let's suppose, too, that the children are new charges for you. You never have been in this house before, or at least are not familiar with the house and its routine. A good baby sitter would do these things first:

1. Get acquainted with the children, if you don't already know each other. Do it while their mother is still there. It pays to allow time to do this.

2. Find out from the parents, and write down, the telephone number where you can reach them in case of any emergency.

3. Find out from the parents, and write down, the name and telephone number of this family's doctor. Some sitters like to have the name and telephone number of a nearby neighbor who would help out if needed. If you must reach the police or fire de-

partment or utilities companies in an emergency, the telephone operator will give you their numbers.

4. Find out the location in this house of telephone, light switches, bathroom, stove (if you plan to use it), heating system or heater, and the location of all outside doors.

5. Find out where the children's clothing is kept, and where towels and sheets are stored.

6. Find out the children's schedule—mealtime, any homework for the older children, where the children are supposed to play or nap.

7. If you are to serve a meal, find out what the children are to eat.

8. Ask the parents, or the mother, exactly what your duties are. Are you expected to prepare a light supper? Take the family dog out for a walk along with the children? Better write things down.

9. Ask what your privileges are. May you use their radio or television set? May you use their telephone for a necessary personal call? (Keep it brief, please.)

TAKING CARE OF CHILDREN BEFORE BEDTIME

Most baby sitting jobs are for a few hours before the children's bedtime. Sometimes ("If you're lucky," says my friend, Midge Fortune) the mother already has put the children to bed by the time you reach their house. That's not always the case, however.

One of the best ways to persuade children to go to bed eventually is to allow them to play for an hour or so first, depending on their ages. If they have a pleasant, full afternoon or evening, they will be sleepy when bedtime comes. Don't let them become overtired or overexcited, though. Use your good judgment.

GAMES TO PLAY

What games do you know? If you have one child, a very young child, to take care of, there are guessing games in which you try to guess what he had for breakfast, what is in his pocket, or he tries to guess what you have hidden in your hand. If you are sitting with an older child, you can play pad and pencil games, paper cutouts, or blowing soap bubbles. When you have several children with you, then you have a wide choice of games from Going to Jerusalem to Ghost to everyone's taking a turn at telling a mystery story. With several children you probably will have to allow for differences in ages, choosing games to please everyone. Try charades, Follow the Leader, Hide-and-Seek (with a head start for the smaller players), or acting out a Western movie or TV play you've all seen.

Let the children choose and plan their own games as much as possible. Older children will have their homework to do, too. See that they do it, and still share in the fun.

Simple magic tricks fascinate most children, especially boys. You can buy an inexpensive magic kit which will make any child finally ask you, "How do you do that?" Let him in on the secret. Teach a child to do magic tricks himself.

Riddles and jokes are always fun. So is drawing your own cartoons or caricatures.

Children like to make things. Pipestem cleaners turn into figures or animals. Clothespins can be dressed and painted (with red nail polish) as dolls. Save birthday and Christmas cards for children to look at and make into a picture album. They can make the album, too, or buy one at the ten-cent store. Matching up playing cards or teaspoons of different designs is another simple, but engrossing, pastime.

Pipestem cleaners or clothespin figures are sure to delight your small charges.

GETTING A CHILD TO BED

Now that "your" children are sleepy and tired, approach the subject of bedtime gradually and with diplomacy. Mention that in half an hour it will be time to go to sleep—do the children want to read aloud, or listen to a story, or have a glass of milk and a cookie until it's time? Give them something to do, not too strenuous, and tell them that now you'll turn down the bedclothes and put on the bathroom light for them. Don't hustle a child off to bed without warning—give him time to get ready to sleep.

Sometimes a child needs to be calmed down. If he is hurt or frightened, take plenty of time to soothe and comfort him. If he is overexcited, read aloud to him. Or give him a warm, not hot, bath. Make it fun, with a sailboat or other floating toy in the tub.

Never leave a small child quickly, once he is in bed. Stay and visit with him a little while, with the light on, while he gets settled. Then tell him that you will be nearby, within earshot, if he needs you.

With an older child, agree together on a time when he will go to bed of his own accord. Leave it to him to keep an eye on the clock or his watch. Be diplomatic; don't issue orders. If he is a little late, that's not too important. The main thing is: If you show a child you trust him and depend on him, he will usually cooperate. If he still balks at bedtime, offer him a story or a game once he is in bed. Story-telling is sometimes necessary and it's always a treat.

When you put or help a child to bed, be good-humored and calm. Don't hurry. Remember teddy bears and dolls need to be tucked in for the night, too, as a comfort to their small owners.

Leave doors open between you and the sleeping children. Keep alert. Every half hour or so, look in on the sleeping children to make sure they are covered, have enough air, and are sleeping quietly.

THE CHILD WHO WON'T STAY IN BED

Few children are really willing to go to bed, and when their parents aren't at home, some have difficulty in falling asleep. If a child sings and talks in bed, don't be surprised. If he gets up and comes in to see you, or calls you for a drink of water, don't scold. Probably he only wants to make sure that you are close by and watching out for him. Perhaps, too, he is still too "wound up" to be able to sleep. In that case, escort him back to bed and tell him a bedtime story or sing him a song.

If the child still insists on staying up, don't force him back to bed. Cover him warmly and invite him to sit with you for a little while longer. Or you stay with him until he gets sleepy. He probably isn't being naughty. He is lonesome and a little frightened in his parents' absence. What he needs is reassurance that you are there and that you're his friend. After one more pleasant visit with you, he'll be satisfied and sleepy. Giving him a glass of warm milk and leaving a dim light on in his room are understanding things that you can do for this child.

MEALS FOR CHILDREN

Sometimes you will be expected to serve a simple lunch or supper to the children you are sitting with. More often it will be a snack after school or before bedtime. The children's mother generally leaves food which is prepared or half prepared and which you need only heat up. At times you may make sandwiches or scramble eggs.

Mealtime can be pleasant for the children and for you, too, if you'll make it fun. Let the children help you get the food ready, though you'll remember that the kitchen can be the most dangerous room in the house. Young children had best be delegated to set the table. Ask the children what they'd like to eat, and serve them that, if possible (or reasonable). Simple menus are best for children. Put sandwich makings on the table and let each make his own. Before you sit down together, everybody's hands must be washed and faces clean.

Don't be appalled if your small charges' table manners are less than perfect. Let him eat in his own way, as slowly as he wants. Offer small portions, and don't insist that he finish all the food on his plate. If he won't eat at all, let it go. You can tell him you'll save the food for him in case he gets hungry later. Forcing a child to eat when he doesn't want to eat can give him indigestion.

Children sometimes ask for food between meals. Unless their mother objects, you can offer crackers or a glass of milk or fruit juice. Just a little snack usually satisfies them. Children get thirsty frequently, without realizing it, so remember to offer a glass of water every hour or two.

Like anyone else, children appreciate food which looks attractive. A sprig of parsley and a radish beside a sandwich can seem festive to a small child. An extra touch, especially a sweet touch, is appreciated—a marshmallow floating in a cup of cocoa, or chocolate syrup to dress up a glass of milk.

Serve meals to children at least an hour or more before bedtime. Food renews energy, and drives away sleepiness. This does not apply to a *small* bedtime snack, such as cookies or a glass of warm milk.

You can make mealtime, like bedtime, a happy, relaxed part of the child's day.

GENERAL POINTERS ABOUT TAKING CARE OF CHILDREN

Be patient. Be cheerful. Be firm. Be kind.

Imagine yourself in the child's place, dependent on you for his safety and his happiness. Treat the child as you'd want to be treated yourself.

Use your imagination in other ways. Play with children and enjoy yourself with them, on *their* level. Then they'll like and enjoy you, too.

You can't very well reason with or discipline very young children. You can manage them happily with games and toys, and with love and patience.

Give a child time to get used to you and acquainted with you. Go slowly, talk only a little, be interested in his small world and doings. Admire, but be honest, about it. Often a pat or hug helps more than words. It takes time to earn a child's friendship, because children usually sense what is genuine or what is not in someone older than themselves. It may take you several visits, but a child's friendship is a real compliment, and well worth having.

Taking care of children is such an important subject that it deserves a whole book. Taking care of babies is special and detailed, and is a subject by itself.

DO'S AND DONT'S FOR BABY SITTERS

Don't fall asleep.
Don't close doors.
Don't telephone unless you have to.

Don't bring a crowd of friends with you. You might bring one friend, with the permission of the children's parents. But most sitters prefer to come alone and concentrate on their job.

Bring a sweater, a chocolate bar (for quick energy to keep you awake), a flashlight. And bring games or something else entertaining for the children, even if it's only in your head.

Dress nicely and look pretty for children. It means a good deal to them.

Children come first. Any household chores come second. Skip them rather than neglect the children.

It's all right to do your homework after the children are asleep, or to watch television or listen to the radio *a little*—but your responsibility to the children comes first! Keep checking every half hour or so that they are all right.

In case of fire, get the children out at once and don't try to save anything else.

In case of illness, telephone the family's doctor, then the family.

In case of any emergency, report it at once by telephone. Get help immediately—fastest by telephone. Remember to notify the children's family at once, too. Then go back to the children, reassure them, and stay with them.

If you have a cold or any other infection, don't baby sit until you are well again.

THIS BUSINESS OF BABY SITTING

Did you know there are about six million baby sitters in the United States? More are needed.

Who is this much-in-demand baby sitter? It might be you. She (occasionally he) is a teen-ager with affection and skill for children. Some high schools give courses in baby sitting, with real live youngsters for practice. Forty-eight per cent of America's teen-age girls baby sit.

HOW TO FIND ASSIGNMENTS

Your neighbors who have young children, and who know you to be a responsible person, are the most immediate source of jobs. Ask your neighbors. Some towns and cities have baby-sitting agencies where you can apply for jobs. (An agency which finds you a job is entitled to charge you a portion of your earnings.) Often the people at your church or community center will know of a family that needs a baby sitter.

It's a good idea to be an experienced baby sitter before you offer your services. You can gain experience by working as a volunteer without pay at a nursery school, or by minding your neighbors' children for an hour or so at a time without charge, or by accompanying a baby sitter on her assignments.

WHAT IS A GOOD BABY SITTING JOB?

Your own parents will want to be sure that you are going to the home of reliable people, who will return at the hour they promise, and who will not make unreasonable demands on you. If you have any doubts about the family, don't accept the assignment.

Don't go into a home where there is serious illness, or contagion.

Don't baby sit in a house which is a firetrap, or which is in a very lonely location. (Always know where exit doors are, how they lock and open.)

Before you accept the job, plan on how you will get there from your house, and how you will get home again. Most girls can get to a job on their own, early in the evening. Then their own parents call for them, or the children's mother or father will escort them home. Tiresome but true: don't wander around by yourself, nor even with another girl or two, late at night. Don't accept rides with persons whom you don't know. Always write down for your family the name, address and telephone number of where you are going. These precautions are for your safety.

A good assignment would be one in which your duties are baby sitting only, without household chores or at least just light ones. For example, after giving the children supper, you could wash their dishes. A good assignment would mean taking care of a child or children who are not problems to handle, and whose parents co-operate to make your task easier.

BE BUSINESSLIKE

Charge whatever are the usual rates in your neighborhood. Ask around to find out what these are.

Before you take a job, find out from the mother how many children you will take care of, for what and how many hours, and have it clearly understood what you charge per hour. Write down her instructions in a notebook.

Keep a large, businesslike notebook with the family's names, children's ages, addresses, telephone numbers, dates, hours, rates and special instructions for each of your assignments. Write this information down *before* each assignment. Add for each family the name of their doctor and a neighbor who will help in an emergency.

Try to find, and keep, steady assignments with the same families. The nearer to your own home, the better.

Try to meet the children in advance, so that you won't be a stranger when you sit with them.

CHERRY SAYS

1. If someone does not especially like children, would she make a good baby sitter?
2. What are a baby sitter's main responsibilities toward the children she is taking care of?
3. What can you do to help and please a sick child?
4. What are the first things a good sitter does when she arrives at the children's house?
5. How do you take care of children before bedtime?
6. How do you put or help a child to bed?
7. How do you prepare and serve a meal to children?
8. What is a good assignment? How do you find it?

CHAPTER XX

Your Future in Nursing

TEEN-AGE NURSES' AIDES

IF YOU'D LIKE TO BE A TEEN-AGE NURSES' AIDE IN A hospital—right now—you'll be interested in what the Candy Stripers, the Jugs, the Hi-Tri's and King's Daughters do. These pace-setters, and several other groups, were the first high school girls to help out hospitals where there are not enough nurses. They assist the nurses, help in hospital offices and laboratories, and provide TLC for the patients. (TLC is tender loving care, an important factor in getting well.) And their help is at a near-professional level.

JUDY, ANN, AND COMPANY

Judy R. of New Jersey assists Miss Hall, R.N., on Women's Medical Ward, for two hours after school every day. Besides doing everything Miss Hall hasn't time to do, Judy serves supper trays, helps feed helpless patients, provides drinking water, makes beds, and does the patients' shopping and errands.

Ann B. of Colorado assists Mrs. Blakelee on Men's Orthopedic Ward. She's the R.N.'s extra pair of hands, writes letters for and feeds the patients, and also assists in central supply.

Ginny N. of New York is the most cheerful addition to Women's Surgical Ward in several years, say the doctors and nurses. The patients call her "an angel in bobby socks." When she's needed, Ginny helps to clean up in the operating room—or cares for the patients' flowers.

Claire W. is a highly popular aide on Children's Ward, because she knows what fun it is for a sick child to drink milk out of a bright blue cup or how consoling to take care of a "lost" doll. Kate L. helps prepare special diets in a hospital kitchen, and is becoming famous among the patients for her attractive salads. One of Kate's tasks is to help the dietitian plan a month's menus for the entire hospital. Marjorie C. helps out in the hospital laboratories, working alongside the white-coated technologists. Julie S., in the Admissions and Records office, has helped to put the records into shipshape order, to the vast relief of many hospital staff personnel.

TOO YOUNG?

Fourteen is these girls' average age. Some are older, a few are younger. All are devoted, skilled, and—because of the shortage of nurses—of great value to their hospitals. Hospitals can accept more patients and give them better care when junior nurses' aides come in every afternoon to help. Some doctors say the presence of young, lively, sympathetic aides in their crisp blue-and-white pinafores does the patients as much good as a tonic.

Working as a junior nurses' aide is fun—and it requires a lot of you. It requires more than being a certain age. Have you good health, good judgment, a sense of humor, and a liking for people? Can other people rely on you?

FINDING ANSWERS

Being a teen-age nurses' aide is a good way to learn nursing skills from professionals. You'll learn a lot about dealing with people, too.

Have you ever thought that you might want to become a nurse? Working as a nurses' aide is a practical way to find out whether you really would like nursing as a career or not.

Junior nurses' aides work in groups. You do not apply or start as an individual; you'll see why when we discuss training. High-school girls work in volunteer groups, in their local hospitals, for a few hours weekly after school, or during summer vacations. Some schools give credit. Most of the hospitals give awards —a white nurse's cap, and an achievement pin. In some areas the Red Cross trains junior nurses' aides and supervises them at the local hospital. The Red Cross holds a capping ceremony for its Junior Staff Aides, as it calls them.

In case you are interested in serving at your hospital, you might join a junior nurses' aide group through your church, Girl Scouts, Y or Red Cross. Perhaps a club you already belong to is searching for a good idea for volunteer work. Or you might form a club among the girls you know.

YOU ARE NEEDED

Your help is badly needed. In many hospitals all over the United States, beds stand vacant and sick people remain on waiting lists because there are not enough nurses. Because of this shortage of R.N.'s, there is an urgent need for nurses' aides. Teen-age girls can and do come to the rescue in understaffed hospitals.

YOUR TRAINING

This is the training you and your group will receive. It is professional training, given usually by the hospital Head Nurse. First, a tour of the entire hospital. Then twenty hours of lectures or nursing techniques, over a period of several weeks. After you receive a preventive innoculation, you will choose a job. You may work directly with the patients, or do dietetics in the hospital kitchens, or assist with X-ray and biochemical tests in the hospital laboratories. You may serve in the offices and information center, or if you're good at arts and crafts you may work with patients for occupational therapy.

YOUR TEAM

You'll work in teams, when you work with patients. Your team consists of the Ward Head Nurse, the

R.N. ward nurse, a practical nurse, and you. Your *special* job—besides your regular job—is to provide tender loving care—particularly for children—to do errands, write letters for patients, and be cheerful young company.

YOUR UNIFORM

You'll wear a bright-colored, washable pinafore with a white blouse. The Candy Stripers wear blue-and-white striped pinafores, for instance. Some girls earn the cost of their uniforms at the hospital. In a few cases the hospitals pay for the cost of the uniforms, which is modest in any case.

YOUR REWARDS

Occasionally junior nurses' aides are paid, but most of the girls work as volunteers, contributing their services for the good of their community.

Your rewards as a nurses' aide can be very special —the personal reward of a job well done. When you see your bedridden patients get well and walk out of the hospital—when you stop and talk with someone on the street who is well because *you* helped nurse him or her—well, there's no other greater reward.

DO YOU WANT TO BE A NURSE?

If any girl thinks being a nurse means chiefly wearing a fetching cap and uniform, and adventuring among romantic people, she is mistaken. (Story books notwithstanding!) Nursing is hard work, a day-in-and-day-out responsibility. Some of it is drudgery like scrubbing up. It takes great patience, stamina, kindness and selflessness. It takes poise, judgment, self-reliance. Nursing does not pay great sums; nurses are well-paid but they do not enter the profession because they hope to grow rich.

The girls and women who take care of the sick, and who help keep well people well, come to their work in a spirit of unselfish service and dedication. They really care about people. They feel that the contribution a nurse can make is beyond price; that is part of her reward, too. They know that a nurse will always be respected and needed wherever she goes, and that nursing is a secure, lifetime profession.

Girls can both become nurses and plan to marry and raise families. A nurse, when her children are grown, can almost always return to her profession part- or full-time, after a refresher course, because nurses are so much needed.

TRY YOURSELF OUT

Before you choose a profession, nursing or any other, you'd be wise to sample that profession first. For nursing, working as a junior nurses' aide is of course one ideal way. If there are home nursing courses given at your local Red Cross or Y or in your school, it's a good idea to take them, too. In case there are none for your age group, you could ask your School Nurse to give a course in home nursing.

FUTURE NURSES' CLUB

If you would like advice on nursing as a career, write to The Committee on Careers, of the National League for Nursing, 2 Park Avenue, New York 16, N. Y. They will also advise you, if you wish, on how to form a Future Nurses' Club.

PRE-NURSING COURSES

If you plan to become a nurse, you must take the appropriate courses in high school. As a rule these are biology, chemistry, biochemistry (if offered), and hygiene. Later on when you work with doctors, you may find frequent use for Latin and mathematics, though these subjects are not usually required. A cookery course is useful for a future nurse. Don't forget that a nurse is a companion to her patients—a great variety of people!—and must have a well-stocked mind. You'll use and enjoy courses in English, history, music, and the other liberal arts subjects. That is, a college preparatory course in high school is advisable.

Your school teacher or grade advisor can tell you what courses you should take to be qualified to enter a first-rate nursing school. Or you may write, again, for advice to The Committee on Careers, of the National League for Nursing, 2 Park Avenue, New York 16, N. Y.

For a good nursing school to accept you, you must be a high-school graduate, aged eighteen, or in some schools, seventeen. You must have good grades, preferably in the upper half of your class. Some nursing schools require you to have completed one to four years of college studies. You must also take and pass a thorough health examination.

GOOD NURSING SCHOOLS FOR R.N.'S

To locate a good nursing school, you may write to The Committee on Careers, of the National League for Nursing, 2 Park Avenue, New York 16, N. Y. (This is a branch of The American Nurses Association, to which almost all our nurses belong. The ANA helps nurses and their patients, improves the standards of nursing schools, gains better salaries and working hours for the profession, and recruits student nurses.)

Ask the Committee on Careers for their list of nursing schools in your area, or in various parts of the country. They will send you up-to-the-minute information about the hospital with which the nursing school is affiliated, in some cases its college or university affiliation, its size, costs, time required to complete its courses, and any other information you might need. Then write to the school or schools where you'd like to apply.

A good school will be approved by the State Board of Nurse Examiners in its state, and by the Accrediting Service of the National League for Nursing.

Hospital schools offer a three-year nursing program leading to your diploma and license as a Registered Nurse.

Collegiate schools offer a four-to-five-year program of nursing, *plus* college subjects, leading to a B.S. or B.A. and your diploma and license as a Registered Nurse.

Once you are licensed as an R.N., you are qualified to do general staff nursing. If you wish to specialize, you'll take advanced courses *after* graduation from either hospital or collegiate nursing school.

PRACTICAL NURSE TRAINING

If you are interested in becoming a practical nurse, write to the National Association for Practical Nurse Education, 654 Madison Avenue, New York, N. Y. and ask for a list of accredited schools and courses. A practical nurse receives in-service training in a hospital, for nine to eighteen months, depending on what her state requires. For example, New York State requires one year of training. Massachusetts requires fifteen months.

Something new in high schools is a course in practical nursing. You'll spend a six-week period training in a hospital, plus a six-week period in high-school classroom and laboratory study, plus work in-training one summer in a hospital. This adds up to complete training. That is, when a girl graduates from high school, she can qualify as a practical nurse. So far, New York is the only state to offer this vocational high school course, but educators in other states are now considering it.

If you are interested, write to your State Education Department, Vocational Division, in your state capital. Ask whether any high school near you has or soon will have a course in practical nursing.

The entrance requirements in New York State for courses in practical nursing are graduation from an eight-year elementary school course. New York State plans to raise the requirement soon to two years of high school training, either academic, commercial or vocational.

SCHOLARSHIPS AND COSTS

The Committee on Careers, whose address I've already mentioned, will be glad to send you a list of nursing scholarships for which you may apply. Quite a few are available. There are also loan funds for students.

Scholarships for practical nurse training are offered by some individual high schools, and by Rotary and other service clubs. Ask at your school, especially your School Nurse, and in your community groups.

Tuition fees and other costs vary in different schools. Some schools will charge you a modest fee for your uniforms, books, and supplies, and not charge you at all for tuition. Other schools charge from $100 to $500 a year for the courses. Collegiate nursing schools charge from $500 to $2,000 a year.

AT NURSING SCHOOL

Most nurses will tell you that their years in nursing school were the gayest of their lives. And that's in spite of intensive programs in classrooms, labs, plus nursing practice in the school's affiliated hospital.

Your courses include anatomy, physiology, micro-biology, psychology, nutrition, medical and surgical nursing, nursing of babies and children, community health, and many other vital subjects. The majority of girls enjoy most that part of their day when they assist the R.N.'s on the hospital wards—or help operating nurses in Surgery, after having witnessed several operations in an amphitheater—or work in Out-Patient or Emergency Wards alongside the graduate hospital staff. You soon become part of a medical team. You can't help but learn and grow up at a hospital nursing school.

When I was at Spencer Nursing School, with all the good friends I made there, the Student Nurses Residence Hall was home—as it is in every nursing school. Every girl has an attractive sitting-bedroom; in some schools, two girls may share a room. There's a small kitchen you may use on each floor, cheerful dining rooms, lounges where you may entertain your family and friends, chapel, and a library. For time off, there are proms, picnics, sports facilities, and the Head Nurse's teas.

Probationers wear no cap for their first three months at nursing school. Then, if their work is good, they receive their caps in a capping ceremony. All student nurses wear striped uniforms, and black shoes and stockings. Only the graduate nurse, the R.N., is privileged to wear white from head to foot, and (in some hospital schools) a black band on her cap.

NURSES' CAPS

Have you ever noticed what a fascinating variety of nurses' caps there are? Each hospital awards its own distinctive cap to its graduates. In this way you can tell where a nurse has taken her training. The "frilled cupcake" of Philadelphia General Hospital was the first style of nurse's caps to be awarded in the United States, when the school started in 1885.

SPECIAL FIELDS OF NURSING

Do you like babies? Pediatric nursing is a highly skilled field, and babies' nurses are in great demand.

Have you a flair with children? You may decide to "special" as a child's nurse, doing your nursing in hospitals or in private homes or wherever you are called.

Within hospitals, some nurses specialize in Operating Room techniques. Some are floor nurses, and their work is largely administrative. Some nurses who are trained for particular cases, like tuberculosis or cardiac conditions, are called into hospitals or private homes to "special" a case—that is, give special, private nursing care.

Private duty nurses may travel. Other nurses who *do* travel are those in the U. S. Army, Navy, and Flight Nurse Corps—three distinct corps. On U. S. Indian reservations you'll find specially educated nurses; theirs is a Federal appointment. In factories and plants, you'll meet industrial nurses and her assisting nurses. There they teach accident prevention and run a general health clinic right in the factory. Visiting nurses go into people's homes to nurse and to teach families good health practices. Public health nurses teach entire communities through big public institutions. You already know about school nurses

Beth Israel Hospital
New York, N.Y.

Kings Co. Hospital
Brooklyn, N.Y.

Fanny Allen School of Nursing
Winooski, Vt.

U.S. Navy Nurse

Abbott Hospital
Minneapolis, Minn.

Little Jolly School of Nursing
Houston, Tex.

Good Samaritan Hospital
Lexington, Ky.

St. Luke's and Children's Med. Cen.
Philadelphia, Pa.

Dillard Univ. Hospital
New Orleans, La.

Leonard Morse Hospital
Natick, Mass.

Boston City Hospital
Boston, Mass.

New York Hospital,
New York

St. Catherines Hospital
Brooklyn, N.Y.

NURSES' CAPS

Cupcakes, starched triangles, black-banded crescents—
each nursing school proudly presents its own distinctive
cap to its graduating student nurses.

and the nurses who assist in doctor's offices. Department store nurses—clinic nurses—nurses who are teachers and administrators—psychiatric nurses—nurses who operate nursing homes—nurses who nurse and teach in little-known areas of South America, of Africa, of Alaska—the list could go on and on.

Whatever a nurse's special field, she honors her nurse's pledge: to serve wherever and whenever another human being needs her.

Postscript

Now that we have discussed so many topics about nursing and good health, you can see, I'm sure, how important nursing is—to you as an individual, to your family, and to your community. For good health is the foundation of everything else in our daily lives.

We can't all be nurses of the greatness of Florence Nightingale who, under conditions of extreme hardship, set the standards of modern scientific nursing—nor as famous as such other pioneer nurses as Clara Barton, founder of the American Red Cross; Sister Mary Joseph who with two physicians, the Mayo brothers, founded the Mayo Clinic in Rochester, Minnesota; Lillian Wald, founder of the Visiting Nurse Service of New York; and Mary E. P. Mahoney, the first Negro professional nurse who established the first Negro nurses' association.

Some of us will become professional nurses. Others of us will be good first-aiders and good home nurses, whenever we are called upon to help. Any girl can expect to give a great deal of home and health care, and unselfish service, to her family and community during the course of her lifetime. Perhaps that is why there is a saying that nurses—and girls with a knowledge of nursing—make the best wives and mothers and the best homemakers.

I hope that you have enjoyed reading and using this book, and that it will be a good friend to you.

Cherry Ames